THE ADVENTURE OF HOLINESS

BY THE SAME AUTHOR

The Pilgrim God: A Biblical Journey
(Washington: The Pastoral Press, 1985/Dublin: Veritas, 1990)

The Way of the Lord: A New Testament Pilgrimage
(The Pastoral Press/Veritas, 1990)

Praying the Our Father Today
(The Pastoral Press, 1992)

God of the Unexpected
(London: Geoffrey Chapman/Mowbray, 1995)

Visit our web site at
WWW.ALBAHOUSE.ORG

The Adventure of Holiness

Biblical Foundations and Present-Day Perspectives

BROTHER JOHN OF TAIZÉ

ALBA·HOUSE house NEW·YORK

SOCIETY OF ST. PAUL, 2187 VICTORY BLVD., STATEN ISLAND, NEW YORK 10314

ST PAULS

Originally published in French by Ateliers et Presses de Taizé,
Taizé-Communauté, France under the title *L'aventure de la
sainteté - fondements bibliques et perspectives actuelles.*

Library of Congress Cataloging-in-Publication Data

John of Taizé, frère.
    [Aventure de la sainteté. English.]
    The adventure of holiness: biblical foundations and present-day
perspectives / John of Taizé.
        p.   cm.
    Includes bibliographical references.
    ISBN 0-8189-0877-7
    1. Holiness.   I. Title.
    BT767.J5513   1999
    234'.8 — dc21   99-28261
                                                 CIP

Produced and designed in the United States of America by the
Fathers and Brothers of the Society of St. Paul,
2187 Victory Boulevard, Staten Island, New York 10314-6603,
as part of their communications apostolate.

ISBN: 0-8189-0877-7

Printing Information:

Current Printing - first digit   1   2   3   4   5   6   7   8   9   10

Year of Current Printing - first year shown

1999 2000 2001 2002 2003 2004 2005 2006 2007 2008

Contents

Introduction

A book on holiness? Whatever for? If there is one topic
that seems tailor-made not to excite the enthusiasm of the
masses, this could well be it. In perpetual motion, our
world offers an ever larger panoply of activities, at least to
those who are not forced to stand outside the gates of the
Palace of Abundance (and the excluded are more
numerous today than ever before). Human possibilities
have never been as extensive as they are now; it seems
only a matter of time before the last enemies of life —
sickness, hunger, decrepitude — will be eliminated by the
scientific and technical mind. Tolerance keeps gaining
ground: the broad commingling of civilizations that
marks the end of our century makes us less and less
disposed to judge those who think or act differently. Even
if exclusive tendencies still appear here and there, it is
easy to interpret them as retrograde phenomena that will
soon be engulfed by the tidal wave of a liberal and
liberated society. Tell me, then, whatever makes you think
that a topic like holiness could interest our well-fed and
satisfied contemporaries, and especially the younger
generations, so eager to accumulate every possible
experience?

But perhaps the general picture that has just been sketched out does not offer a comprehensive vision of our present situation. What if our infatuation for all forms of entertainment were, in the final analysis, simply a gigantic attempt to conceal a generalized and deadly boredom that threatens to swallow everything we have attained? What if our tolerance were only the other side of a deep-seated indifference: since "it's all the same," why waste time and energy trying to defend a particular point of view? Is it conceivable that behind the facade of an efficient and successful civilization there lurks the specter of nihilism, all the more terrifying since it remains unavowed? We keep running, dancing and shouting, and the music must never stop, for we live in mortal fear that in the resulting silence we will hear only emptiness, the relentless ticking of the clock of our mortality.

Sixty years ago, the French writer Georges Bernanos already described this situation in his novel *The Diary of a Country Priest:*

> ...the world is eaten up by boredom.... It is like dust. You go about and never notice, you breathe it in, you eat and drink it. It is sifted so fine, it doesn't even grit on your teeth. But stand still for an instant and there it is, coating your face and hands. To shake off this drizzle of ashes you must be for ever on the go. And so people are always "on the go."[1]

Bernanos likewise understood the spiritual roots of this state of affairs:

> Perhaps the answer would be that the world has long been familiar with boredom, that such is the true con-

---

[1] Georges Bernanos, *The Diary of a Country Priest* (New York: The Macmillan Company, 1954), pp. 1-3, for this and the following excerpts.

dition of man. No doubt the seed was scattered all over life, and here and there found fertile soil to take root; but I wonder if man has ever before experienced this contagion, this leprosy of boredom: an aborted despair, a shameful form of despair in some way like the fermentation of a Christianity in decay.

It is not a question of ascertaining whether the present epoch is better or worse than another. Each age has enough troubles of its own. Our task is to comprehend the challenges and the dead-ends of today, in order to find ways to go forward. Otherwise the generosity and good will of so many of our contemporaries, especially the youngest, are in danger of leading nowhere, like clear mountain streams that sink into oblivion in swampland.

Already one thing is clear even to the most superficial observer: our world no longer offers a global vision able to integrate all the domains of life into a harmonious whole. This development is not entirely negative; it is, in part, a reaction against an earlier unity now sensed as incomplete, as excluding or disfiguring whole portions of reality. In the progress of the human spirit, the breakdown of earlier syntheses as a result of new discoveries is the necessary prelude to new attainments. But breakdown in itself is not progress, and life is no picnic for those born in an age of fragmentation.[2] Post-mod-

---

[2] My suspicion is that the most glowing apologies of cultural anarchy and fragmentation come from those who grew up in an earlier age, where the reigning mental categories had almost completely lost touch with new realities and had hardened in a last-ditch attempt to hold back the rising tide of what was perceived as chaos. These individuals thus experienced breakdown as essentially liberating. It is a far different story for those who have known nothing but relativism, and whose search for solid ground under their feet is generally caricatured by their elders as mere reaction or fundamentalism.

ern society is a society shattered into bits; its problem is not so much a lack of meaning as an infinity of meanings with no obvious relationship among themselves. It is consequently up to each individual, using the most disparate fragments of meaning at their disposal, to craft an identity that seems to work, in essence to reinvent the world. If this state of affairs favors tolerance and great flexibility, to such an extent that some are already celebrating the new "protean self,"[3] it cannot be denied that it engenders beings who are fragile, easily disoriented, lacking a strong backbone. Inner unity seems an impossible dream and, in some cases, the temptation is great to exorcize the anguish by imposing a narrow, sectarian unity, thus replacing the missing backbone with a hard shell.

In fact, we are beginning to realize that boredom and fragmentation are spiritual diseases, which therefore require remedies of the same order. From his obscure parish, our country priest even glimpsed the way out:

> My parish is bored stiff.... I had never been so horribly aware both of my people's loneliness and mine. I thought of the cattle which I could hear coughing somewhere in the mist, and of the little lad on his way back from school clutching his satchel, who would soon be leading them over sodden fields to a warm sweet-smelling byre.... And my parish, my village seemed to be waiting too — without much hope after so many nights in the mud — for a master to follow towards some un-dreamed-of, improbable shelter.
> Oh, of course I know all this is fantastic. Such notions can scarcely be taken seriously. A day-dream! Villages

---

[3] This is the title of a book by Robert Jay Lifton, *The Protean Self: Human Resilience in an Age of Fragmentation* (New York: Basic Books, 1993).

do not scramble to their feet like cattle at the call of a
little boy. And yet, last night, I believe a saint might have
roused it....

This is the conviction that animates the present work: the
only way out of the current crisis of confidence in humanity
will involve a rediscovery of the holy. An arduous enterprise,
almost an insane one, when we contemplate to what extent
our society has lost touch with its spiritual roots. Modernity
has bequeathed to us a world without mystery, where everything is prey to the curiosity and the manipulation of research-
ers who are rarely disinterested. Far from being the sacrament
of a Presence, nature has become a mere raw material, entirely
at our disposition and therefore open to all the ravages of an
unbridled technology. The pollution of our cities and our
countrysides is only a consequence of this, the symptom of a
much deeper imbalance.

Similarly, because "nothing is sacred," we are defenseless
in the face of a suicidal mechanism: we end up destroying what
we love. Since human beings cannot live without objects of
their desire and their admiration, and since at present they
feel obliged to create these objects themselves or, what comes
to the same thing, to endow them with importance, it is not
surprising that they become aware of their Achilles' heel more
and more quickly. They then take a morbid pleasure in cast-
ing down into the mud what they had exalted up to the stars
just a short while before.

How did we reach this point? The answer to this question must be a nuanced one. As we shall see, the Bible itself
presents a masterly critique of a certain conception of holiness, navigating between two extremes: holiness as a diffuse,
depersonalized energy, and holiness as separation. Through
the coming of the Son of God as one of us, the movement of

personalization of the holy was brought to its culmination. At the same time, the wall of separation between the divine and the human was definitively torn down, and "fear" in its negative sense left behind once and for all (cf. 1 Jn 4:18).

Nonetheless, every advance in our comprehension of spiritual realities can open the door to new misunderstandings. In one sense, the biblical and post-biblical critique of pagan holiness did its job too well. If the Judeo-Christian revelation disenchanted the world, draining off all holiness from the cosmos in order to condense it in a personal God, the Creator of heaven and earth, then where faith in this God began to disappear, all that remained was a disenchanted world. In eliminating the fear of a wrathful God, it also unwittingly promoted a weakening of the sense of mystery and of the mind-boggling depths of reality in favor of a hygienic universe, a kind of Disneyland of the spirit.[4] And the activistic mentality of the Western world, heirs to the organizational genius of Rome but too often lacking in depth, instigated a notable drift toward moralism and legalism which has influenced the entire Christian Church in the West. As a result, for most of our contemporaries the word "holy" has lost

---

[4] A certain Christian theology, present and past, has tended to downplay the category of the "fear of God," considering it as a vestige of an infantile or pernicious religiosity, incompatible with the God of love. In so doing this theology amputates an essential aspect of its message and dooms itself to insignificance. A technological society where a superficial efficiency reigns can quite easily accommodate a watered-down faith where love is reduced to a tame benevolence, without passion. As I shall try to make clear in these pages, the solution does not consist in a rejection of "fear of the Lord" but in its interpretation in the light of Jesus Christ. If God is Love, then there is no reason to be afraid *of God*. But the encounter with such an unconditional Love is indeed fearful insofar as it unsettles the very foundations of the human condition, notably all the excuses by which we attempt to conceal our own refusals to love and be loved: "But with you is forgiveness, and so you are feared" (Ps 130:4).

all mysterious or mystical connotations and has simply come to stand for an ethical heroism, or even a ludicrous sanctimoniousness.

It should come as no surprise, then, that in a functional high-tech society the sacred is returning in a big way from the outside, especially via different forms of Eastern spirituality. From a certain point of view, what is called New Age is nothing other than the return of repressed aspects of holiness into the collective consciousness of the Christian and post-Christian West. And as always when repressed material comes back into consciousness, it is both a warning and an opportunity. It shows us how urgent it is for the civilization which arose from the Judeo-Christian tradition to return to its roots, by deepening the vision of the holy found in the Hebrew Scriptures as well as in the New Testament. When this is done, an authentic discernment can take place. We can discover what we can learn from non-biblical spiritualities, and what needs to be reoriented or perhaps even rejected in the light of Christ. A true encounter between religions, desired by many at this dawn of a new millennium, cannot dispense with this discernment.

The starting-point of this book was a series of Bible introductions on the theme of holiness, given over two years in the context of the international meetings that bring tens of thousands of young adults to the hill of Taizé each year. Those who listen to these introductions are very diverse in terms of their knowledge of the Bible and their faith-commitment. In coming to Taizé, they are not only looking for information about the wellsprings of the Christian faith but also desire an experience of that faith, made concrete in prayer and community life. This explains the particular style of these introductions, midway between exegesis and spirituality. There is also present a concern, for pedagogical reasons, to weave a coherent story. I am not unaware of the diversity of the theologies found in the pages of Scripture, but it has seemed preferable to me to place the accent on the continuity of the biblical teaching, emphasizing its unity so that its originality can better be grasped.

In addition, I am convinced that biblical theology should not be afraid of an element of anachronism, for often a reality of faith is only correctly understood in the light of what follows. It is the fruit that permits us clearly to identity the seed and the tree (Lk 6:43-44). And we should not forget that for Christians, in the final analysis it is Christ in his death and resurrection who sheds full light on all the dark corners of the self-revelation which God has undertaken down through the ages.

Why, then, a book about holiness? When all is said and done, to stimulate reflection on a topic able to restore flavor to a world which, in spite of all its impressive acquisitions on the level of knowing and doing, runs the permanent risk of sinking into insipidity. And capable of offering a basis upon which can be built a unity fully respectful of the diversity of existence, because it is rooted in a soil which is not of this world. Are these claims excessive? Let them rather be seen as a call to an ardent and confident fidelity in the One who has promised to make us the salt of the earth and the light of the world. We will now set out to look for that seasoning and that flame, by meditating on the pages of that source of life we call the Bible.

Abbot Lot came to Abbot Joseph and said,
"Father, according as I am able,
I keep my little rule,
and my little fast, my prayer,
meditation and contemplative silence;
and according as I am able
I strive to cleanse my heart of thoughts.
Now what more should I do?"
The elder rose up in reply
and stretched out his hands to heaven,
and his fingers became like ten lamps of fire.
He said,
"Why not be totally changed into fire?"

From the sayings of the "Desert Fathers,"
fourth-century Egyptian monks

Biblical Abbreviations

OLD TESTAMENT

Genesis	Gn	Nehemiah	Ne	Baruch	Ba
Exodus	Ex	Tobit	Tb	Ezekiel	Ezk
Leviticus	Lv	Judith	Jdt	Daniel	Dn
Numbers	Nb	Esther	Est	Hosea	Ho
Deuteronomy	Dt	1 Maccabees	1 M	Joel	Jl
Joshua	Jos	2 Maccabees	2 M	Amos	Am
Judges	Jg	Job	Jb	Obadiah	Ob
Ruth	Rt	Psalms	Ps	Jonah	Jon
1 Samuel	1 S	Proverbs	Pr	Micah	Mi
2 Samuel	2 S	Ecclesiastes	Ec	Nahum	Na
1 Kings	1 K	Song of Songs	Sg	Habakkuk	Hab
2 Kings	2 K	Wisdom	Ws	Zephaniah	Zp
1 Chronicles	1 Ch	Sirach	Si	Haggai	Hg
2 Chronicles	2 Ch	Isaiah	Is	Malachi	Ml
Ezra	Ezr	Jeremiah	Jr	Zechariah	Zc
		Lamentations	Lm		

NEW TESTAMENT

Matthew	Mt	Ephesians	Eph	Hebrews	Heb
Mark	Mk	Philippians	Ph	James	Jm
Luke	Lk	Colossians	Col	1 Peter	1 P
John	Jn	1 Thessalonians	1 Th	2 Peter	2 P
Acts	Ac	2 Thessalonians	2 Th	1 John	1 Jn
Romans	Rm	1 Timothy	1 Tm	2 John	2 Jn
1 Corinthians	1 Cor	2 Timothy	2 Tm	3 John	3 Jn
2 Corinthians	2 Cor	Titus	Tt	Jude	Jude
Galatians	Gal	Philemon	Phm	Revelation	Rv

THE ADVENTURE OF HOLINESS

Approaching
the Mystery

1   There are words and expressions whose meaning
seems obvious until you start to think about them. The
word "holy" is a good example. For many people today,
the term refers above all to a moral quality of a human
being. The following definition from the *Collins English
Dictionary* is a good example: "Holy: devout, godly or
virtuous." Such a starting-point, however evident it may
seem, sets us on the wrong road from the very outset.
Before we can deal with the question of holiness in
human beings, we need to make a long detour. A
glance at the history of religions will convince us that it
is better to begin by considering holiness as a reality
outside human beings, a reality with which they are
confronted in the course of a particular *experience.*[1]

---

[1]   In speaking of holiness as an experience, I am not trying to limit it or to
distinguish it from other ways of perceiving reality, as for example
Martin Buber does in his well-known book *Ich und Du* (1923, Eng. trans.
I and Thou, New York: Charles Scribner's Sons, 1970). The Jewish
scholar distinguishes between *Erfahrung* ("experience"), which he sees
as characteristic of an I-It relationship, and *Beziehung* ("relationship"),
characteristic of an I-Thou relationship. In these pages I use the word
experience in a very global way, simply to mean that something
happens to someone that they themselves have not produced and that
has consequences for their life. The word "event" could also be used.

1

Such experiences are found in many different civilizations. In the Bible, a particularly telling example is given in the life of Moses, in the third chapter of the Book of Exodus. In this event which will deeply mark him for life, we have what could be called an archetypal experience of the human encounter with holiness.

Chapter two of the Book of Exodus informs us about the life of Moses before this key event. Born in Egypt as a Hebrew and thus a member of an oppressed class, the baby Moses was discovered by the king's daughter and raised as an Egyptian. He thus grew up with a double identity; today some might try to interpret his history in terms of an "identity crisis." In any case, it seems clear that the young Moses was not fully at home in the world he saw around him; he felt the need for a radical change. He tried to create a more just society, but this attempt led only to failure. Having killed a man, he was forced to flee for his life.

And so, in chapter three, we find Moses far from home, "an alien in a foreign land" (Ex 2:22). Now a shepherd, one day he leads his flock into the wilderness off the beaten track. There, far from the life of organized society, something happens to that uprooted man which enables us to discover the basic aspects of the experience of holiness:

> Now Moses was tending the flock of Jethro his father-in-law, the priest of Midian, and he led the flock to the far side of the desert and came to Horeb, the mountain of God. There the angel of the Lord appeared to him in flames of fire from within a bush. Moses saw that though the bush was on fire it did not burn up. So Moses thought, "I will go over and see this strange sight — why the bush does not burn up."
> When the Lord saw that he had gone over to look, God called to him from within the bush, "Moses? Moses?"

And Moses said, "Here I am."
"Do not come any closer," God said. "Take off your sandals, for the place where you are standing is holy
ground."
Then he said, "I am the God of your father, the God of
Abraham, the God of Isaac and the God of Jacob." At
this, Moses hid his face, because he was afraid to look
at God.   (Ex 3:1-6)

The experience of Moses begins with a "strange sight"
(NIV, NJB), a "great sight" (NRSV), in other words the encounter with something unexpected and unsettling, although
rooted in simple elements of creation. A bush is on fire, without being burnt up. This unusual phenomenon is like a road
sign that points the way out of our normal universe towards
another level of being. Put another way, it is like a question
mark that opens the door to an unknown world, whose laws
are not those which govern ordinary life.

A word sometimes used to characterize such a phenomenon is the word *mystery*. But here, instead of referring to a
mere enigma, a problem to be solved or a question to be an-
swered, the term indicates a reality that bears an inexhaust-
ible meaning. A mystery is a kind of gateway to a universe in
constant expansion, where the more discoveries you make the
more there is to learn. It is a crisis-point where the ordered
surface of the cosmos breaks open, offering a glimpse of fath-
omless depths. And the image of fire emphasizes the dynamic
quality of a mystery; it is not mere passivity, but a reality ani-
mated by its own life.

In the face of this mysterious reality, Moses' reaction is
complex, even paradoxical. First of all, he comes closer: "I will
go over and see this strange sight..." (v. 3). In an experience
of mystery there is something that attracts, that fascinates. In
the depths of someone's being a thirst is awakened, one which

that person had never before known. In this respect, the experience of holiness resembles the encounter with beauty: a
human being is drawn spontaneously towards a reality that
seems to him attractive and meaningful.

At the same time, another reaction quickly becomes evident. Moses hears a voice tell him, "Do not come any closer"
(v. 5). And then we read, "Moses hid his face, because he was
afraid to look at God" (v. 6b). Paradoxically, the experience
of mystery awakens both the desire to come closer and the fear
of getting too close. By covering his face, Moses attempts to protect himself from a reality that has a threatening aspect to it.

Let us try to understand better this second aspect of
Moses' reaction. Exactly what kind of "fear" does he feel? It is
not, first of all, the fear of punishment, nor a fear of being
annihilated by an evil power: it is significant that the fire does
not destroy the bush. The "fear" Moses experiences is of a
totally different order; it is closer to a fear of the unknown. It
expresses the state of mind of a person who leaves behind his
everyday world and who is confronted with something absolutely new and unexpected, a powerful reality whose laws he
does not know and after which he will never be the same
again.[2]

If this second dimension is likewise a basic characteristic
of the experience of holiness, it is equally true that it can vary
greatly according to the situation. In front of the burning bush
Moses' fear is not too oppressive, since he does not run away
and the encounter continues. Later, however, when he returns
to the same mountain together with the Israelites liberated

---

[2] For an interpretation of the Bible which takes as its starting-point the theme
of newness see Brother John of Taizé, *God of the Unexpected* (London:
Mowbray/Geoffrey Chapman, 1995). The two notions of newness and holiness shed light on each other.

from slavery, the experience of holiness during a violent storm is so terrifying that the people refuse to come any closer:

> When the people saw the thunder and lightning and heard the trumpet and saw the mountain in smoke, they trembled with fear. They stayed at a distance and said to Moses, "Speak to us yourself and we will listen. But do not have God speak to us or we will die."
>
> (Ex 20:18-19)

Such experiences lead the people of the Bible to the conclusion that one cannot have a direct encounter with God's holiness and remain alive (Ex 19:21ff; 33:20; 1 S 6:20). It should be emphasized once again that this in no way implies that God is not well-disposed toward human beings — the God revealed on Mount Sinai is the same God who freed the Israelites from oppression and is leading them to a land of happiness — but rather that, in their frailty, creatures are not made for an encounter with absolute Reality. In Exodus 33:18-23, for example, Moses for his part wishes to see God, who attempts to dissuade him from such a rash undertaking.

At the other extreme, the "fear" which arises from the experience of holiness can take on the guise of a respectful attentiveness or an astonishment mingled with awe, or even of stupefaction. The variations are endless and the vocabulary quite rich, but the important thing is to grasp the essence of the experience in question: the encounter with a mysterious and dynamic reality which both satisfies the deepest thirst of human beings and impels them towards another plane of existence which calls into question the very foundations of their life.[3]

---

[3] Despite the passing of the years, the phenomenological study of holiness made by the German theologian Rudolf Otto *(Das Heilige,* 1917; Eng. trans. *The Idea of the Holy,* New York: Oxford University Press, 1958) is not at all

The act Moses is asked to perform when he encounters the burning bush emphasizes another important aspect of the experience of holiness: "Take off your sandals, for the place where you are standing is holy ground" (Ex 3:5). In biblical times, when someone bought a field, the first thing they did was to walk around it. This was a way of expressing that they were officially taking possession of the territory. To step on something, especially if we are wearing shoes or boots, is a quite natural way of saying, "This is mine. It belongs to me. I am the proprietor."

The fact that Moses is required to take off his sandals before walking on the ground where the burning bush is means that, by definition, something holy can never be possessed, manipulated or controlled by human beings. They are entering a realm where they are not the ones in charge, where all they can do is let themselves be welcomed. The attitude required is one of respect for what is given, of giving up control. This characteristic of mystery sheds additional light on the "fear" or awe we have been speaking of. Human beings are obviously ill-at-ease in a situation where they are not the masters and where their basic vulnerability comes to light. And we can better understand why the experience of holiness appears particularly incongruous in the modern world, to such an extent that it is literally incomprehensible to many of our contemporaries. A technological and scientific civilization reduces a mystery to a mere problem to be solved. Far from removing their sandals, its representatives outfit themselves

---

outdated. It is evident that these pages are deeply indebted to his notion of *mysterium tremendum et fascinans*. For another investigation of holiness that considers less the subjective consequences than the diversity of objective manifestations, see G. Van der Leeuw, *Religion in Essence and Manifestation* (Princeton University Press, 1986). Cf. also the writings of Mircea Eliade.

with all kinds of "shoes" in order to investigate phenomena and to extract what is useful. Notwithstanding the undoubted advantages it offers in the realm of practical life, such an attitude makes an authentic encounter with the reality of holiness practically impossible.

When confronted with holiness, a traditional society is likewise not fully at ease. There, however, we find a different way of dealing with the problem. It consists in isolating the holy place or thing from the rest of life, by erecting visible or invisible walls around it. So, for example, rules are established which limit the access to certain times, or to certain persons who have first satisfied certain conditions. These "laws of purity" seek to respond to different exigencies. In the first place, they are an attempt to protect human beings from a redoubtable power that "disturbs" ordinary life because it is not subject to its laws. But in addition, since the bearer of holiness (stone, tree, place…) is at the same time an object belonging to this world, there is always the danger of profaning it. The laws of purity thus also strive to protect the holy object from an encroachment that would cause it to lose its holiness. We can sum up this development in a word by saying that "the holy" tends to become "the sacred." This is even reflected in the etymology of the vocabulary of holiness: in Hebrew, the word "holy," *qodesh*, comes from a root that also means "separate, set apart."

The world of the Bible is not unaware of this tendency to isolate a holy reality. As in many other civilizations, the concern for ritual purity left its mark in Israel as well. This is only to be expected, since Israel always lived in symbiosis with the surrounding world. The revelation of the One who alone is God does not come down from heaven ready-made: God's activity, by its very nature, slowly transforms human and earthly realities so that they can express his designs. As far as holiness is concerned, we will see that the aspect of separation, however comprehensible and even necessary it may have been at certain times and places, does not express its fundamental significance. On the contrary, the notion of separation represents in the final analysis an obstacle to an authentic understanding of biblical holiness.

Let us now look, for purposes of comparison, at another experience of holiness recounted in the Bible, one that took place several centuries after the time of Moses. It occurs at the very beginning of the career of Isaiah, the man who will be one of the greatest of Israel's prophets:

> In the year that King Uzziah died, I saw the Lord seated on a throne, high and exalted, and the train of his robe filled the temple. Above him were seraphs, each with six wings.... And they were calling to one another: "Holy, holy, holy is the Lord Almighty; the whole earth is full of his glory." At the sound of their voices the doorposts and thresholds shook and the temple was filled with smoke. "Woe to me!" I cried. "I am ruined! For I am a man of unclean lips, and I live among a people of unclean lips, and my eyes have seen the King, the Lord Almighty."   (Is 6:1-5)

Whereas Moses was an outsider wandering in the wilderness, far from human society, Isaiah is at the center of Israel's public life, in the great Temple of Jerusalem. One day, presumably during a liturgical celebration, the prophet had an experience of holiness, a vision of the Lord as a great king surrounded by splendor. Heavenly beings were singing his praises and the Temple was filled with smoke. As in the case of Moses, Isaiah encountered a mystery that was beyond him and left him breathless. In the Song of the Seraphs (v. 3b), we find an important word from the biblical vocabulary of holiness. It is the word *kabod,* generally translated as "glory." It comes from a root meaning "that which has weight" and refers to the outward expression of the reality of a being. Here, it expresses the fact that holiness is a dynamic reality which radiates outward, spreading to fill the entire universe. In a word, God's glory is the radiance of his holiness.

Confronted with this imposing vision, Isaiah also has a backward movement. In his case, though, the experience is a more inward one. What he feels is not so much fear as the sentiment of how fragile and imperfect he is. "A man with unclean lips," he considers himself unable to take part in the heavenly singing. The contact with holiness awakens in him the feeling of not being up to the mark. Compared to the overflowing life he encounters, he experiences himself as someone not fully alive.

Questions for Reflection

1. The Bible shows us that the fact of being far from home can be a privileged situation for encountering God. Have I had such "desert experiences" in my life? When and how? What can we do in order not to bring Egypt with us into the wilderness?
2. When we begin to look more closely, we discover that in the course of their existence many people have had an experience of the mystery of life. Such experiences are a good starting point to understand what Moses and Isaiah went through. Personally, have I had any such experiences in the realm of nature (mountains, sea, sunset...), art (music, poetry...), human relationships (intimacy, friendship, service...), prayer (the beauty of a liturgy...)?

3. Like Isaiah, have I discovered God's presence in everyday life with others, for instance in my local church, as well as in exceptional times and places? Do I sometimes feel unqualified to undertake what God is asking of me? How do I deal with this?

A Consuming
Fire

2

In the last chapter, we began to deepen our
understanding of the word "holy" in the Bible. We
started from the notion of holiness as a particular
experience a human being can undergo: the
encounter with a mysterious reality charged with
energy. This reality both attracts and frightens, since it
pulls humans away from the banality of daily life and
draws them into a new and unknown world.

In the Bible texts where Moses and Isaiah have such an
experience of holiness, we find something which
functions as a classical symbol or image of holiness in
many different religious traditions. This image is *fire*.
An enigmatic and dynamic phenomenon, fire is both
fascinating and menacing; human beings are drawn to
it yet are unable to come too close. Beautiful and
useful, it is not without danger, because it easily
escapes human control. For all these reasons, fire is a
natural symbol of holiness.

In the Bible, there are countless texts in which the
image of fire is found. We will now examine some of

them, as a way of deepening our understanding of different aspects of holiness. In the oldest layers of the Bible, the coming of the divine into our world is often described in very concrete terms by the use of dramatic images of natural upheavals, for example a storm, an earthquake or a conflagration. The technical term given to this kind of manifestation is the word *theophany* ("appearance of God"). We have already mentioned in passing the theophany on Mount Sinai:

> On the morning of the third day there was thunder and lightning, with a thick cloud over the mountain, and a very loud trumpet blast. Everyone in the camp trembled. Then Moses led the people out of the camp to meet with God, and they stood at the foot of the mountain. Mount Sinai was covered with smoke, because the Lord descended on it in fire. The smoke billowed up from it like smoke from a furnace, the whole mountain trembled violently, and the sound of the trumpet grew louder and louder.   (Ex 19:16-19a)

These violent phenomena express the upheavals caused by the entry of the divine into the world here below. It is a dramatic way of indicating that creation is incapable of "containing" God, that God's presence disturbs the rhythms of a universe always tempted to view itself as autonomous. But this coming of God is not purely or essentially destructive. Most of the time, God reveals his presence in this way, in fire and storm, in order to combat in favor of his people. In Psalm 18, for example, the king is threatened and calls upon the Lord, who comes to save him:

> In my distress I called to the Lord;
> I cried to my God for help.
> From his temple he heard my voice;

my cry came before him, into his ears.
The earth trembled and quaked,
and the foundations of the mountains shook....
Smoke rose from his nostrils;
consuming fire came from his mouth....
He parted the heavens and came down;
dark clouds were under his feet....
Out of the brightness of his presence clouds advanced,
with hailstones and bolts of lightning.
(Ps 18:6-12)

In these archaic or seemingly archaic texts (cf. also Jg 5:4-5; Ps 68:1-2; 97:3-5), to save his people God becomes present in the upheavals of nature. Even if, at a later date, the necessary link between such natural phenomena and the coming of God will be called into question (cf. 1 K 19:11-13), it is significant that, from the beginning, the image of fire is spontaneously associated with the presence of the deity.

Another aspect of the image of fire is shown during the pilgrimage of God's people in the desert after their departure from Egypt:

By day the Lord went ahead of them in a pillar of cloud to guide them on their way and by night in a pillar of fire to give them light, so that they could travel by day or night. Neither the pillar of cloud by day nor the pillar of fire by night left its place in front of the people.
(Ex 13:21-22)

Here, the fire manifests its beneficial side; it sheds light so as to show the way to go (cf. Ps 18:28; 119:105). And Jesus in his turn will take up this image when he says, "I am the light of the world. Whoever follows me will not walk around in the darkness, but will have the light of life" (Jn 8:12).

It is not surprising that the book of the prophet Isaiah, marked so deeply by the vision of God as the Holy One of Israel, is particularly rich in these texts. Starting from the notion of fire as a reality that cleanses, that eliminates what is useless or dangerous, the prophet expresses his conviction that the presence of Holiness in the midst of the nation which he glimpsed in his inaugural vision will finally lead to a purification:

> The Light of Israel will become a fire,
> their Holy One a flame;
> in a single day it will burn and consume
> his thorns and his briers.
>
> (Is 10:17)

And then, all who are identified with evil will feel that they have been singled out; for them, a healthy awe will turn into the terror of being annihilated:

> The sinners in Zion are terrified;
> trembling grips the godless:
> "Who of us can dwell with the consuming fire?
> Who of us can dwell with everlasting burning?"
>
> (Is 33:14)

But this fear of destruction is far from being the last word. Without hesitating, the prophet answers his own question:

> Those who walk righteously
> and speak what is right,
> who reject gain from extortion
> and keep their hands from accepting bribes,
> who stop their ears against plots of murder
> and shut their eyes against contemplating evil....
>
> (Is 33:15)

The image of a purifying fire becomes a call to conversion, an urgent invitation not to cling to realities destined for destruction, to behavior that will not resist the approach of holiness. Isaiah thus shows us the roots of what is destined to undergo a long development in the Bible under the rubric of "the fire of judgment" or "God's anger." But when these themes are detached from a global vision of holiness, their true significance no longer becomes apparent. In the mouth of preachers who confuse their own darkness with a divine mission, they only serve to foster unhealthy guilt-feelings in the mind of their hearers. The "fire of holiness" (need it be said again?) does not aim to destroy; simply, by its nature it is incompatible with evil. The only things doomed to be lost definitively are those which prohibit God's loving designs from being realized:

> Every warrior's boot used in battle
> and every garment rolled in blood
> will be destined for burning,
> will be fuel for the fire.
>
> (Is 9:5)

A later prophet describes, in his turn, God's entry into his Temple as a cleansing fire. Here the purification is meant above all for the priests, making them finally able to present offerings pleasing to God:

> See, I will send my messenger, who will prepare the way before me. Then suddenly the Lord you are seeking will come to his temple....
> But who can endure the day of his coming? Who can stand when he appears? For he will be like a refiner's fire or a launderer's soap. He will sit as a refiner and purifier of silver; he will purify the Levites and refine

them like gold and silver. Then the Lord will have
people who will bring offerings in righteousness....
"Surely the day is coming; it will burn like a furnace. All
the arrogant and every evildoer will be stubble, and that
day that is coming will set them on fire," says the Lord
Almighty. "Not a root or a branch will be left to them.
But for you who revere my name, the sun of righteousness will rise with healing in its wings."
(Ml 3:1-3; 4:1-2; cf. Zc 13:9)

In the prophet's eyes, one and the same manifestation
of the divine will be a conflagration that devours for some and
a sun that warms and heals for others.

Finally, another series of texts describes fire as something
that protects. The day will come when God's glory, glimpsed
during the Exodus, will make its home permanently in the
midst of the nation, protecting Israel from its enemies and
preserving it from cosmic upheavals:

> Then the Lord will create over all of Mount Zion and
> over those who assemble there a cloud of smoke by day
> and a glow of flaming fire by night; over all the glory
> will be a canopy. It will be a shelter and shade from the
> heat of the day, and a refuge and hiding-place from the
> storm and rain.   (Is 4:5-6)

It would not be difficult to prolong this list of Bible texts
that use the image of fire to describe the characteristics of
holiness. But this suffices to show the importance of the image and the diversity of its applications. God's fire is one, although it has different consequences according to the situation. It is something that purifies, that protects, that illumi-
nates, that shows the way, that cleanses, that shelters... but it
is always the same reality. From the side of God everything is

simple; the complexity comes from the diversity of human situations.[1] The fire of holiness, in its encounter with our human world, causes a host of different effects which should not let us lose sight of the underlying unity. This same mystery is expressed in the words of a song that recapitulates the basic intuition of a seventh-century monk, known as Isaac of Ninive: "All God can do is give his love."

Question for Reflection

1. When the author of the Letter to the Hebrews takes up the words of Deuteronomy: "Our God is a consuming fire" (Heb 12:29; Dt 4:24), is he communicating good news? In what way? Is he contradicting the great affirmation of Saint John: "God is Love" (1 Jn 4:8,16)? If there is no contradiction, then what does the image of fire add to our understanding of love?

---

[1] Cf. the remarks of Blaise Pascal: "Everything which does not lead to charity is figurative. The sole object of Scripture is charity. (...) God diversified this single precept of charity to satisfy our curiosity, which seeks diversity, through a diversity which always leads us to the one thing that is necessary for us. For, while one thing is necessary, we like diversity, and God meets both needs by this diversity which leads to the one thing necessary." (*Pensées* 270, trans. A.J. Krailsheimer, Penguin Books, 1966, 1995, pp. 83-84).

A God
Who Speaks

3 In examining the notion of holiness as a particular
experience accessible to human beings, as an
encounter with a reality that both attracts and
frightens, we have taken two examples from the
universe of the Judeo-Christian Scriptures. At the same
time, a glance at the history of religions shows us that
similar experiences occur in other civilizations as well.
A particularly noteworthy example is this theophany
found in the Bhagavad Gita, one of the classics of
Hindu spirituality:

> O King, saying this, Krishna,
> the great lord of discipline,
> revealed to Arjuna
> the true majesty of his form....
> If the light of a thousand suns
> were to rise in the sky at once,
> it would be like the light
> of that great spirit....
> Then filled with amazement,
> his hair bristling on his flesh,
> Arjuna bowed his head to the god,

joined his hands in homage, and spoke.
I see you blazing
through the fiery rays
of your crown, mace and discus,
hard to behold
in the burning light
of fire and sun
that surrounds
your measureless presence....
the moon and sun in your eyes,
your mouths of consuming flames,
your own brilliance
scorching the universe.
You alone fill the space
between heaven and earth
and all the directions;
seeing this awesome,
terrible form of yours,
Great Soul,
the three worlds
tremble.[1]

To point out such a resemblance does not, however, imply the claim that "all religions are identical." First of all, because by emphasizing common features, we provisionally neglect differences of detail which can have extremely important consequences. But especially, because a religion cannot be reduced to an experience. Having an experience is one thing; understanding it and integrating it into the whole of

[1] Bhagavad Gita XI: 9, 12, 14,17, 19, 20. *The Bhagavad Gita: Krishna's Counsel in Time of War.* A translation by Barbara Stoler Miller (New York: Columbia University Press, 1986). It should be noted in passing that the Bhagavad Gita is not the simple transcription of a spiritual experience "in the raw" but rather a well-constructed literary work. This does not exclude the likelihood, of course, that an authentic spiritual experience lies at the origin of the text.

life is another. An experience in itself is only a starting point. In the final analysis, it is the *meaning* that we attribute to it that will matter for our spiritual life: its origins, its consequences, its links with the rest of life. What matters finally is the place a reality that is out of the ordinary occupies in the life of society and of the individual.

Now it is obvious that the religious traditions of humanity differ greatly in the way they regard the meaning of the experience of holiness. Let us take, for example, the aspect of fear that we have identified as a basic element of the experience. This reaction can be interpreted as the response to an evil power — or at least one that is not well-disposed — ready to destroy human beings, a power that must therefore be propitiated by appropriate means. In that case, apprehension in the face of the unknown will shift more and more in the direction of a servile fear. Similarly, one people may emphasize the tendency to isolate the holy object or place, another the desire to enter into contact with it. Thus either fear or attraction can gain the upper hand. These possibilities, and many others, are not just theoretical, as can be seen by the great diversity of religious practices and beliefs that punctuate the history of our planet.

For this reason, an experience as such is above all a question that calls for an answer. In the domain that interests us here, this question can be expressed in the following way: What significance does the Bible attribute to holiness? How does the physiognomy of this reality become more and more precise through the unique history of God's people told in the Hebrew Scriptures, and in the life of Jesus Christ?

To answer these questions, let us return to the story of Moses at the burning bush, reading it in a way that allows the specific nature of biblical holiness to stand out. When Moses began to move closer to the bush, we read:

> When the Lord saw that he had gone over to look, God
> called to him from within the bush.   (Ex 3:4a)

This fire is unlike any other; it has a voice. In other words, it is not an object but a subject; it witnesses to a personal reality that we call God.

If this seems evident or even banal to us, that is because we are influenced, perhaps unwittingly, by the Judeo-Christian revelation. But the history of humanity offers us many other ways of viewing holiness. For many Eastern spiritualities as well as some contemporary ones, holiness is basically impersonal: it is a kind of energy. The basic conviction is that ultimate reality is something beyond persons with all their limits, that a personal mode of being represents an obstacle to true universality. It is true that, in the Bible too, holiness is something dynamic, an "energy" or force capable of transforming the face of the earth. The fact that we have forgotten this, reducing holiness to a rather effete moral quality, explains in large part the attraction of exotic spiritualities for many of our contemporaries.

But if holiness is necessarily a transforming power, for the Bible this dynamism is neither anonymous nor blind; on the contrary, it bears a personal name.[2] This explains the horror with which the Bible considers anything that comes close to a magical vision of the world. A magician plays with blind

---

[2] These pages do not examine the question whether the notion of holiness refers to the deity taken in itself or whether it describes the creature's encounter with the world of the divine. It is perhaps in part a question of definition: are we considering the experience in itself, or rather what makes it possible? Let us just mention in passing that Christian theology in both East and West makes a distinction between God as he is in himself and as he is in his relationship to humanity. The Eastern Church distinguishes between the incommunicable *essence* of God and his deifying *energies*. The Western Church speaks of *uncreated* grace (the Holy Spirit) and *created* grace (the Spirit's effects in human life).

forces, thinking he can control them if only he can discover the rules of the game. For biblical faith, however, all these impersonal manifestations are only the outer garments that simultaneously hide and reveal a Face. Holiness is thus not, in the final analysis, a characteristic of the objects themselves but the expression of a *relationship*. The universe is revealed as sacramental, in other words permeable to a transcendent dimension.

Behind the experience of holiness there thus lies a personal reality, a God who speaks. Speaking means going outside of oneself to communicate something to someone else — a message, a meaning. The God of the Bible, far from being a potentate shut up in his "splendid isolation," a mere goal of our searching or an object of veneration, is someone who sets out in quest of his creation in order to share his life.

We are perhaps too used to the notion of a God who speaks to appreciate its full significance. The expression "the Word of God" applied to the Bible may lead us astray, for it necessarily makes us think of a book, of words written or printed on a page. In reality, that is not the main thing: behind the transcribed word is the act of a God who speaks, in other words who communicates. And most of the time, this communication does not take place primarily through human words. At the time of the Bible, just as today, God has a great many different languages at his disposition. God speaks through human beings and through the events of our lives; God speaks to us in the depths of our heart when we pray. Then, when we try to understand and communicate to others what God says to us, we are obliged to translate it into a human language, whether discursive or symbolic. But in general this only comes later, as a second stage.

Very early, God's people became aware of this characteristic of its God. When the leaders of Israel, exiled in Babylon, were faced with the imposing statues of the Babylonian deities, they made fun of them by saying: "They have mouths, but cannot speak" (Ps 115:5; 135:16; cf. Jr 10:5). Our God, on the other hand, may be invisible, but he speaks to us.

This particularity of the God of Israel also has its drawbacks. Listening to the voice of the living God is far from being a comfortable experience. We have already mentioned the people's fear during the theophany on Mount Sinai (Ex 20:18-19). The book of Deuteronomy explains this in greater detail:

> When you heard the voice out of the darkness, while the mountain was ablaze with fire, all the leaders of your tribes and your elders came to me. And you said, "The Lord our God has shown us his glory and his majesty, and we have heard his voice from the fire. Today we have seen that people can live even if God speaks with them. But now, why should we die? This great fire will consume us, and we will die if we hear the voice of the Lord our God any longer. For what mortal has ever heard the voice of the living God speaking out of fire, as we have, and survived?"   (Dt 5:23-26)

Once again, the Israelites do not imagine here that God is their enemy; they are well aware that God freed them from slavery in Egypt and is leading them to a land of plenty. Nonetheless, a direct encounter with the Holy One awakens fear, uprooting people from the universe they know and opening before them an unknown world where they are no longer in control.

In the story of the burning bush, we do not simply read that God spoke to Moses but that he *called* him. Now to call means much more than simply to speak. Someone who calls does not intend above all to transmit information but rather to invite the listener into a relationship. If the God of the Bible speaks to us, that is in the final analysis because he wishes to enter into a relationship, a dialogue, with those he has created. And in so doing, God runs a risk. Whoever calls appeals to the freedom of the one called. That person can listen or not listen, understand the other's language or not understand it, and above all respond or not respond. Here we are far from the mechanical universe of constraint. The God who speaks, or better still who calls, is at the opposite extreme from a deity who manipulates his subjects, a puppet master who pulls strings. The God who calls, by that very fact, wishes for beings who respond intelligently and freely to the call.

Seen from this angle, the story of the burning bush offers us the basic outline of all of biblical history. From the beginning, God has tried to let his call be heard by the human beings he created (cf. Gn 3:9). God looks for beings able to recognize his voice. And, little by little, because God continues to speak, a listener comes into being who is able to understand this language and to respond. A comparison with human life can help us here. Newborn infants do not immediately understand the words that adults speak to them. And yet, that does not keep people from constantly speaking to babies and calling them by their name. And it is precisely the fact that we speak to them that makes it possible for them one day to understand us and to reply. The encounter with speech awakens in the listener the capacity to speak. Now God acts towards us in much the same way: with infinite patience, God speaks to us in the course of the ages. And finally, one day there appears in the world someone like that Servant described by the prophet Isaiah:

> The Sovereign Lord has given me an instructed tongue,
> to know the word that sustains the weary.
> He wakens me morning by morning,

wakens my ear to listen like one being taught.
The Sovereign Lord has opened my ears,
and I have not been rebellious;
I have not drawn back.   (Is 50:4-5)

The characteristic of God's activity is that it "wakens" the
ear of his partner. And because he has learned to listen in this
way, the Servant can speak in God's name to his contemporaries, translating God's language into human words. The
Word of God is thus able to come down from heaven and to
take its place in human history. It would be more accurate to
say, however, that the first word addressed to us by God goes
back much farther; it is identical to the act by which God created us. The first chapter of the Book of Genesis presents an
incredible notion for anyone who takes the time to think about
it: a God who creates the universe in the act of speaking. In
other words, the very first word God speaks to us is that by
which he "calls us into existence" (Rm 4:17). Translated into
human words, it is as if God were saying to each of us when
we were created: "I want you to exist; I choose you; I love you."
The notion of a Creator God means that the simple fact of
existing contains within it unsuspected depths. It is the beginning of a dialogue, the expression of a meaning that is communicated through a relationship.

Question for Reflection

1. Read Exodus 3:1-15. What do we learn about God from
   this passage? What are the different responses Moses
   makes to God? In what ways do I identify myself with
   Moses?

Called
By Name

4 In the Bible, the encounter with that reality *sui generis* which we call holiness leads to the discovery of a personal God, a God who speaks. And this God calls human beings to begin a dialogue with him, to enter into a reciprocal relationship. But the text of Exodus 3:4 gives us an additional detail: "God called to him from within the bush, 'Moses! Moses!'" From the midst of the fire, God calls Moses by his *name*.

In today's world, names do not play a very important role. When a child is born, naturally parents think a bit about the question. Should we call the newborn infant after its grandmother, or a movie star, or simply give it a name we like? This is generally not of the utmost importance. The name we bear is implicitly regarded as arbitrary; it has only an extrinsic link with the person.

In traditional societies, and that includes the world of the Bible, the situation is quite different. Names are exceedingly important. Never just a word or a label, they are part and parcel of the thing or the person they qualify. That is why in these societies it is not customary to reveal one's name to just anybody. Often, too, people use different names according to the degree of closeness of the relationship, with the most personal name being kept for those with whom one is most intimate. Revealing one's name means handing over a part of oneself to others; it therefore makes us vulnerable.

More precisely, a name in a traditional society is the revelation of what the thing or person in question really *is*. To use a modern expression, the name of a being is his or her or its *identity*. At the same time, since we do not give our name to ourselves and, more often than not, it is used by others to call us, the name expresses a relationship. Here we already see a theme that we shall have an opportunity to develop at greater length in these pages, namely, the link between personal identity and relationships with others.

If all names are important in the world of the Bible, this is all the more so when the name is given directly by God or by a divine messenger. The name given by God, our Creator and consequently the one who knows us better than we know ourselves (cf. Ps 139), reflects who we are in the deepest part of our being; it expresses our truest identity. In addition, it situates this identity in the context of God's overarching plan. The name given by God indicates the project for which God calls a person, their mission in life.

In the first chapter of the Gospel according to Saint Luke, God announces through a messenger the birth of two children. And each time, the announcement is immediately followed by the bestowal of a name:

> The angel said to him, "Do not be afraid, Zechariah, because your prayer has been heard. Your wife Elizabeth will bear you a son and you will name him John...."

> The angel said to her, "Do not be afraid, Mary, for you
> have found favor in God's eyes. See, you will conceive
> and give birth to a son, and you will name him Jesus."
> (Lk 1:13,30-31)

The event of birth is not complete until a name has been revealed and given, in order to situate the newborn child in the human world where God is present and active: *Yohanan* (John), in other words "the Lord shows favor" and *Yeshua* (Jesus), "the Lord saves." In the parallel passage in Matthew's Gospel, the angel explains to Joseph the meaning of the name: "...you will name him Jesus, for he will save his people from their sins" (Mt 1:21).

More often in the Bible, though, God does not give a name to a newborn child but rather to someone already living in the world. The name bestowed by God usually follows an encounter with the Lord which gives a new direction and meaning to life. The encounter leads to a kind of new beginning by which someone is sent out. The new name ratifies this mission and expresses the new identity given by God. For example Abram, after the covenant which God makes with him, becomes Abraham, "father of many" (Gn 17:4-5). For his part the patriarch Jacob, at a critical moment in his life, has a rather unusual experience of the holy God. He does not encounter the Lord in fire or during a storm, but in a nighttime struggle with a mysterious stranger. After this night spent wrestling with the unknown voyager, we read:

> The man asked him, "What is your name?" — "Jacob,"
> he answered. Then the man said, "Your name will no
> longer be Jacob, but Israel, because you have struggled
> with both God and human beings and have overcome."
> (Gn 32:27-28)

This mysterious encounter marks the patriarch for life
and gives him a new identity. When he, in turn, wishes to learn
the name of his assailant, he receives no clear answer. Jacob
has understood, however: "I saw God face to face" (Gn 32:30).
And already his new name, Israel, had revealed this secret
indirectly, containing as it does the divine name "El." Still
Jacob, like countless other human beings across the centuries
when confronted by the unsettling Mystery of life, looks for
greater certainty, something he does not receive. The only way
to "possess" God is to journey in his company (cf. Gn 28:15).

In the Bible, the new name given by God also expresses
a hope for the future. Speaking of the restoration of Jerusalem at an undetermined future date, an anonymous prophet
preaching just after the exile in Babylon cries out:

> The nations will see your righteousness,
> and all kings your glory;
> you will be called by a new name
> that the mouth of the Lord will bestow....
> You will be called Hephzibah ("My-delight-is-in-her")
> and your land Beulah ("Married").
> (Is 62:2,4)

On that day, the true identity of the faithful people will
be made known; it will consist essentially in a relationship to
its Lord. The last book of the Bible takes up this prophecy and
universalizes it:

> To the conqueror I will give... a white stone, and on the
> stone will be written a new name, known only to the one
> who receives it.   (Rv 2:17)

All who remain faithful to God till the end (that is the
meaning of the word "conqueror" in the Book of Revelation,

see Rv 2:26) will ultimately discover through this relationship their most personal identity.

If Moses is called by name from the midst of the fire of divine holiness (Ex 3:4), then, this means that whoever enters into a relationship with the holy God sets out on a road where they will become fully themselves, where little by little they will discover their true face. It should be clear how different this way of seeing is from our own: for many of our contemporaries, one must first discover or become oneself, and only then can one enter into a relationship with others or with God. The Bible turns this way of thinking on its head, and tells us that only through our relationships with others can we become fully ourselves. The principle of individualism is thus radically undermined and the foundations of communion laid.

In speaking to Moses from the burning bush, God does not only call him by name, but reveals the divine Name as well. Here God goes a step further than in the nighttime encounter with Jacob. If it is permissible to express it in human terms, we can say that God decides to run a risk, because he knows that no authentic relationship is possible without reciprocity, without mutual vulnerability.

In fact, in this story God reveals two different names. The main one is given in reply to Moses' request, when God sends him to Pharaoh in order to obtain his people's freedom. Aware of his limits, Moses hesitates and asks for a guarantee, a divine Name he can hide behind and whose power he can make his own. Although God accedes to this request, the reply is not exactly what Moses had in mind. The Name above all names which he communicates to Moses (*'ehyeh 'asher 'ehyeh*, Ex 3:14) is extremely difficult to translate and to interpret, but that is undoubtedly part of its significance! An ordinary name demarcates a being, traces limits around it and situates it within a particular category, in effect saying "I am this" or "I am that."

The Name revealed to Moses, however, situates God beyond all our human categories. That is God's secret: God is precisely the One who calls us out of the prison of our all-too-human routines and limits.

The Name "I am who I am" (or: "I am the one who is" or "I will be who I will be," etc.) emphasizes the sovereign liberty of God, who cannot be manipulated magically or used to prop up a "party line." It evokes as well God's compassionate solidarity; in Hebrew, the verb "to be" includes a connotation of being present and active (cf. v. 12: "I am" with you). God thus reveals himself as infinitely close to human beings in their need, but never at their disposition. In a word, this Name presents God as the Holy One.

The fact that the God of the Bible is beyond all the limits of our world also implies that this God alone can enter into a relationship with the whole human being. In the ancient world there was a great plurality of gods: the god of war, the god of peace, the gods of the household, and so on. People called upon these gods to satisfy particular needs concerning one part of their life. The ancient world had trouble reconciling holiness and unity. There was a strong tendency to consider each great manifestation of holiness as absolutely unique, with no intrinsic relationship to any other. This conviction led members of traditional societies to speak of the spirit of this tree, the god of that mountain, the tutelary deities of this nation. And then a whole mythology would evolve in the course of time to explain the relations between all these different gods — their alliances, their oppositions, their hierarchy. Here diversity is taken for granted, while unity is problematic.

In the Bible we find nothing of this sort. The God who enters into a relationship with Moses is Someone who is situated outside all these partial domains and speaks to human beings from a "place" beyond all the divisions of their being.

A relationship with this God thus makes the unity of the personality possible. Since God's realm takes in the whole of existence, it becomes possible to respond by a yes that commits one's entire being without mutilation. The diversity of existence is thus placed at the service of a deeper unity.

The Bible has a term to speak of a human being seen globally, starting from the center: the *heart*. In the Bible, the heart does not refer to one part of the being, for instance the emotions; it stands for the *whole* being considered from its deepest point. When we say that the God of the Bible is a God who speaks to the heart, we are proclaiming that in a relationship with this God a human being finds true unity. Responding to God's call leads to a gradual unification of a person's life. Slowly but surely they become able to love the Lord with all their heart, all their soul and all their strength (cf. Dt 6:5).

The second name that God reveals to Moses confirms and completes this portrait. "I am the God of your fathers — the God of Abraham, Isaac and Jacob" (Ex 3:6,15). If, in a distant past, each of the great ancestors of the nation had an experience of holiness, sometimes expressed by a particular name,[1] Moses learns that behind all these experiences can be found the same personal reality, the same God he is encountering today. Thus a true historical continuity is made possible, because there is a Reality that transcends all these specific experiences and unifies them. The existence of one God thus goes hand in hand with the beginning of history understood as a succession of events that bears a meaning, and not just a mere insignificant flux.

---

[1] Among others, the God of the mountain or the Almighty Lord (*El Shaddai*, Gn 17:1), the Everlasting God (Gn 21:33), the God who sees me (*El Roi*, Gn 16:13), the Terror of Isaac (Gn 31:42, 53), the Mighty One of Jacob (Gn 49:24). It is likely that, in pre-biblical times, the ancestors of Israel had not yet clearly grasped the unity among all these manifestations of the deity. But in the Bible itself, all we encounter are vestiges of this diversity.

To indicate this historical continuity the Bible uses the word *faithfulness*. The God of the Bible is faithful, in other words always there for his followers. Without this fidelity, no true relationship is possible. This is already obvious in our human world. If I know that another person will not change their feelings toward me from one day to the next, I have the impression that there is solid ground under my feet upon which a lasting relation can be built. Faithfulness gives birth to trust, the basis of every authentic relationship.

The two divine names revealed to Moses thus reveal the indispensable bases of the relationship which God wants to create with human beings. It is not an accident that they appear again in the last book of the Bible, the Book of Revelation, fused into a single expression: "The One who is, who was and who is coming" (Rv 1:4, etc.). This God who stands above this-worldly existence is literally inconceivable, and must take the initiative himself to disclose his identity and his unity. And if human beings can receive God's Name, that means that there is something in them capable of welcoming this revelation and therefore of rising above mere materiality, fragmentation and more or less successful attempts at self-definition. As the Bible puts it, human beings are created in the unimaginable image of God (Gn 1:26).

Question for Reflection

1. Read 1 Samuel 3:1-10. Through what people, events and experiences is God calling me? What keeps me from hearing this call? What can I do to hear it more clearly? Has there been an Eli in my life? How can I be an Eli for others? How do children help us to find God?

Here
I Am!

5 The whole of biblical history is ruled by a great
conviction that distinguishes it from so many other
spiritual paths: for the Bible, God alone is holy (cf. Rv
15:4; 1 S 2:2). In other words, all the experiences of
holiness in their immense variety are not independent,
but witness to one and the same reality. And this reality
bears a personal name; it is "Someone" with whom a
relationship of mutual interiority is possible. In the
story of the burning bush, the voice that comes from
the heart of the fire calls human beings to take part in
a dialogue. The speaker reveals his Name in a sharing
of life through which his partners will discover their
true identity, their own real name.

Let us now look at the words that follow God's call:

> God called to him from within the bush, "Moses!
> Moses!" And Moses said, "Here I am."
>
> (Ex 3:4; cf. Is 6:8)

And Moses said, "Here I am." God's initiative is not
complete until the one called responds to the call. We

must begin by making clear what is meant by a response. In the material world, things are interrelated and so actions have *consequences:* if a spark is struck in a container filled with hydrogen and oxygen in a certain proportion, an explosion will result which will then have other consequences. The human mind can discern in the world a chain of causes and effects.

When we shift to the organic level, we can speak of *reflexes* or *reactions:* the organism itself determines in part the consequences of an action in which it is involved. Thus as the sun shifts in the sky, the leaves of a plant will turn to capture more light. Or when a pet dog hears the sound of a key in the lock at 6 o'clock in the evening, it begins to shake and whine in expectation of its owner's caress and a walk in the park.

Because we are material and organic beings, consequences, reflexes and reactions are also part of the human condition. But human beings have the ability to act on another level as well, to give what can be termed a *response.* A response is situated on the personal level and therefore goes beyond the mere consequences of an action; it likewise differs from a reaction. Far from being a plaything of external or internal forces, whoever responds takes their own life into their hands, so to speak, and takes a conscious and free step that arises from the most personal and inward part of their being. In other words, they assume their destiny and become *responsible:* it is no accident that in most languages the words "response" and "responsible" have the same root.

By its very nature, then, a response cannot be forced. Anyone who chooses to love runs a great risk: they are henceforth suspended on the heart and the words of the other. That is God's "dilemma": God requires our response in order to realize his plan of creation, but he can neither respond for us nor force us to respond. All God can do is to keep on looking for ways of speaking to the human heart, to call us in a host of different ways until the longed-for response is received.

For, however surprising it may seem, human beings do not seem to be built to respond spontaneously when confronted with the divine call. More often than not, they look for *excuses* so as not to hear; they run away from the choice that is offered. Left to themselves, they prefer the security of their habits to the uncertainty of a departure toward the unknown. It is easy to identify this tendency in our life, but we can see it as well in the pages of the Bible. Moses' experience is eloquent in this regard.

In fact, the words "Here I am" which Moses at first speaks express a superficial generosity rather than a well-thought-out decision. When the Lord takes him at his word and sends him to the king of Egypt to ask for the Israelites to be set free, immediately he begins to hesitate: "Who am I, that I should go...." "I will be with you," replies God (Ex 3:11-12). When God sends a person, he always goes along with them. But, Moses continues, "They will ask me in whose name I am coming...." So God reveals his Name (Ex 3:13-15). Then, "What if they do not believe me or listen to me and say, 'The Lord did not appear to you'?" (Ex 4:1). God then gives him two signs to show the others. But Moses is not to be thwarted so easily in his refusal: "O Lord, I have never been eloquent.... I am slow of speech and tongue" (Ex 4:10). To meet this objection, God suggests that he take with him his brother Aaron to be his spokesman.

Here, the human reaction in the face of God's call is demonstrated with all the necessary precision. God speaks and, automatically, his partner continues to set up excuses between himself and the Word in order not to have to take it seriously and assume his responsibility. The prophet Jeremiah, in his turn, will do the same thing when faced with God's call: "Ah, Sovereign Lord, I do not know how to speak; I am only a child" (Jr 1:6). All that God can do, then, is to act with infinite patience, setting aside the excuses one by one and confronting the one called with his or her responsibility.

When a man or a woman, finally leaving their excuses behind them, respond to the divine call to enter into a relationship with God, they are taken up at once into the very same movement which is God's own. God says to Moses:

> I have indeed seen the misery of my people in Egypt. I have heard them crying out because of their slave drivers, and I am concerned about their suffering. So I have come down to rescue them…. So now, go. I am sending you to Pharaoh to bring my people the Israelites out of Egypt.   (Ex 3:7-8a,10)

These words emphasize a characteristic of biblical holiness which is extremely significant. In the religious history of humankind, we have seen that there is an ineluctable tendency to build walls around a manifestation of holiness, to make it sacred; the holy reality becomes something separate, set apart. *In the Bible, however, holiness is revealed more and more unambiguously not as a movement of separation but rather as a "going towards."* In other words, God's holiness leads him to go beyond himself to encounter human beings; it is a reality of communication.

The holy God is above all the one who, attentive to the suffering of his people, comes down to liberate them and to offer them a better life. The story of the burning bush has led us to grasp the truth that, by revealing his holiness, God draws human beings out of their routines and towards an encounter with himself. That, however, is not the end of the story, for God then asks those he calls to enter into the same adventure. A relationship with God is something quite different than a mutual admiration society, a kind of *égoïsme à deux*. It involves being sent out towards others.

In the same way, his own meeting with the Holy One gives the prophet Isaiah an acute awareness of his imperfections. But far from stopping there, the encounter heads toward a further stage. God sends one of his servants to Isaiah to purify his lips with a coal from the altar (Is 6:6-7), thus giving us an eloquent symbol that shows how the fire of God's holiness goes to meet sinful human beings in order to purify them. Thus forgiven, Isaiah is henceforth able to join in the singing of the heavenly choir and he can now receive the mission of speaking to the nation in God's Name (Is 6:8-10).

To the prophet Ezekiel as well, God "shows the holiness of his great Name." He "shows himself holy" (cf. Ezk 36:23), not by a withdrawal but by his activity at the heart of human history:

> I will take you out of the nations; I will gather you from all the countries and bring you back into your own land. I will sprinkle clean water on you, and you will be clean; I will cleanse you from all your impurities and from all your idols. I will give you a new heart and put a new spirit in you; I will remove from you your heart of stone and give you a heart of flesh. And I will put my Spirit in you.... (Ezk 36:24-27a)

Here, God shows himself to be the Holy One above all by forgiving his people, by transforming them from within. Still elsewhere, divine holiness is expressed by the refusal to break a relationship and to punish (Hos 11:7-9), by acts of justice (Is 5:16) or by tender concern for those who are humiliated and wounded (Is 57:15). We are confronted with one of the great paradoxes of biblical revelation: holiness, which in itself indicates God's otherness ("my thoughts are not your thoughts, neither are your ways my ways," Is 55:8-9), appears more and more clearly as the passion for an encounter. It is the movement by which God goes outside himself to speak to human beings, to call them into a communion (cf. Is 55:6-7, 10-11).

Questions for Reflection

1. Read Jeremiah 20:7-11 and Luke 5:1-11. What do we learn about holiness through the experiences of Jeremiah and of Simon Peter?
2. According to Exodus 3:1-15, what is God's response to human beings who doubt their abilities?
3. In what way am I tempted to fabricate a god in my image, either in order to believe in that god or to reject it? What helps us remember that God is always beyond the understanding we have of him?
4. Toward what men and women in need, whose dignity has been wounded, is God sending me? Can I show by the way I live the face of a God who opens a road to life and freedom?

The Grammar
of Holiness

6 Far from being a movement of retreat or separation,
the holiness of the God of the Bible leads him to go out
of himself to seek a relationship with those he created.
And through this relationship with Another, human
beings discover their true identity. Still more, the Bible
reveals to us a God who wishes to communicate his own
holiness to the creatures he has encountered and
liberated.

The Hebrew Scriptures are not, for all that, a collection
of individual histories. The God who is present in them
is not only interested in beings taken one by one. A
personal call finds its full meaning in the context of a
history which is above all the progressive formation of a
people. This people is the primary counterpart of God,
the fundamental bearer of divine holiness.

This is evident in the great theophany on Mount Sinai
(Ex 19 - 20). When the Lord reveals the majesty of his
holiness in cloud, fire and storm, in the presence of
Moses and those who have left Egypt with him, we read:

Then Moses went up to God, and the Lord called to him
from the mountain and said, "This is what you are to
say to the house of Jacob and what you are to tell the
people of Israel: 'You yourselves have seen what I did
to Egypt, and how I carried you on eagles' wings and
brought you to myself. Now if you obey me fully and
keep my covenant, then out of all nations you will be
my treasured possession. Although the whole earth is
mine, you will be for me a kingdom of priests and a holy
nation.' These are the words you are to speak to the Israelites." So Moses went back and summoned the elders
of the people and set before them all the words the Lord
had commanded him to speak. The people all responded together, "We will do everything the Lord has
said." So Moses brought their answer back to the Lord.

(Ex 19:3-8)

The God of holiness turns this band of former slaves into
a people, his own people. To refer to this act of taking them
in hand and thus creating a new actor on the stage of history,
the Bible says that God made a *covenant* with Israel. But there
is more. This covenant makes Israel "a kingdom of priests and
a holy nation" (v. 6). Here we encounter something unique
in the world of that time: holiness characterizes not a place
or an object but a people. In other words, the existence of this
people formed by God will be henceforth a sign of God's presence at the heart of human history. Israel's vocation is to be
above all a "burning bush" that allows all the inhabitants of
the earth to perceive the holiness of its God.

The story of the Sinai covenant emphasizes in addition
that this nation is not holy, and consequently a witness to divine holiness, because of some prior step it has taken to earn
this distinction, but solely because it has been chosen by God
as his "treasured possession" (v. 5). This choice is totally un-

merited; the Bible formally excludes any notion that Israel may have deserved God's care (cf. Dt 7:7-8). At the same time, we are equally far from an automatic or magical understanding of Israel's vocation. The Lord said to them, "If you obey me fully and keep my covenant...," and the people all responded together, "We will do everything the Lord has said" (vv. 5, 8; cf. Jos 24). The nation is asked to consent freely to enter into the relationship offered by the Lord, since the God of the Bible accords no value to the groveling of slaves.

Although Israel is a holy nation solely because of its relationship with the God who alone is holy, it is nonetheless true that this relationship has consequences for the manner in which the people conducts itself day by day. Israel is called to live in such a way that its ongoing life reflects its identity as God's own people:

> The Lord will establish you as his holy people, as he promised you on oath, if you keep the commands of the Lord your God and walk in his ways. Then all the peoples on earth will see that you are called by the name of the Lord, and they will fear you.   (Dt 28:9-10)

This passage gives us a context for understanding the true meaning of the divine commandments in the Bible. In addition, it uncovers the roots of a juxtaposition which will come to be extremely significant, namely, the link between holiness and the ethical dimension of human life. By following "the ways of the Lord," the chosen people works out a lifestyle that is different, that translates the holiness of its God into the concrete realities of its existence. Then the other nations will be able to have the same experience in their encounter with Israel as Moses did before the burning bush: "They will fear you," in other words they will be fascinated and awestruck by a way of life that is unlike any other (cf. Ac 2:43a), that of "people who live apart and do not consider themselves one of the nations" (Nb 23:9).

This logic becomes explicit in one of the component parts of the Torah or Law of Moses, that section known as "the law of holiness" (Lv 17ff.). In these chapters, the principal motivation for observing the commandments is given in this succinct phrase: "Be holy because I, the Lord your God, am holy" (Lv 19:2; cf. 20:26). There follows a series of precepts concerning the recommended way to live one's daily life. And a bit later, the reason for all these requirements is reiterated:

> Consecrate yourselves and be holy, because I am the Lord your God. Keep my decrees and follow them. I am the Lord, who makes you holy.   (Lv 20:7-8)

And here a question arises which is far from being purely theoretical in the world of the Bible. What happens if the people does not live according to the divine commandments? In that case, it becomes a living contradiction; its fundamental identity (who it is) and its concrete life (how it lives) are no longer in harmony. The conclusion of this section of the law of holiness mentions this formidable possibility:

> Keep my commands and follow them. I am the Lord. Do not profane my holy name. I must be acknowledged as holy by the Israelites. I am the Lord, who makes you holy and who brought you out of Egypt to be your God. I am the Lord.   (Lv 22:31-33)

When it no longer follows the Lord's commands, Israel "profanes the holy name of the Lord," in other words it gives the world a false image of God's holiness (cf. Ezk 36:20-23; Is 52:5). That is why Jesus, when he teaches his disciples the great prayer that sums up his message, the "Our Father," begins with the petition "May your Name be made holy." In his eyes, it is essential for believers to pray that their way of life may transmit a true reflection of God and of divine holiness, so that the world may truly see and recognize the face of God.

If God's people expresses its identity as a holy nation by keeping the divine commandments, it is striking to see that a good number of these commandments, gathered together in the first five books of the Bible, deal with the question of worship. It is by "appearing before the Sovereign Lord" (cf. Ex 23:17) in a place of prayer that the Israelites demonstrated from the beginning that they belonged to the holy people. This was already true for the ancestors of the nation (Gn 12:8; 26:25, etc.), then during the Exodus (Ex 33:7-11) and in the early years in the land of Canaan (Jos 8:30-31; 1 S 1:3, etc.). At the time of the monarchy, there was a centralization of worship in the great Temple of Jerusalem, which became for centuries to come the main sanctuary where people went to enter God's presence.

In the life of Israel, prayer is essentially a collective, liturgical reality; the worshiper went to the Temple to pray as part of the entire nation. At this point we encounter the notion of ritual *purity*: Israel, like other cultures, reflected on the necessary conditions required to stand in the presence of the holy God and to take part in the liturgy. We may remember that the prophet Isaiah, when confronted with God's holiness, considered himself impure and therefore unworthy to join in the singing of the heavenly choir (Is 6:5). This fundamental aspect of holiness fostered a reflection by the members of traditional civilizations on the means by which they could become entitled to approach the Source of their life without risk.

The Law of Moses thus contains rules of purification that represent a symbolic language to describe and evaluate access to the holy place and contact with holy objects; they form a kind of "grammar of holiness." In our day, thanks in large part to the ongoing development of the Judeo-Christian revelation, rules of this sort strike us as curious, not to say absurd. Nevertheless, we should beware of rejecting them for the wrong reasons. At best, they are a way of indicating the seriousness of divine holiness and its consequences. If we feel no need for such practices, is that because we have deepened our vision of holiness, or because for us God is no longer a "consuming fire" who gives heat and light to the whole of our existence?

It is likewise true that, already very early in Israel, some people realized that the essential did not consist in outward rites. Psalm 15 asks the question of who can be admitted to the sanctuary:

> Lord, who may dwell in your sanctuary?
> Who may live on your holy hill?
> (Ps 15:1)

Here, incidentally, we have already come a long way from the early days of Israel's faith, because the "holy mountain" referred to is not Sinai but rather Mount Zion, site of the Temple. Then comes the reply:

> Those whose walk is blameless
> and who do what is righteous,
> who speak the truth from their hearts.
> (Ps 15:2ff.)

In this psalm, purity is above all ethical. What makes a person a full member of the holy people is an irreproachable life, conducted according to God's commandments. Psalm 24 goes still further in this direction:

Who may ascend the hill of the Lord?
Who may stand in his holy place?
Those who have clean hands and pure hearts,
who do not lift up their souls to an idol
or swear by what is false.

(Ps 24:3-4)

Here, purity is both a characteristic of the *hands,* in other
words of human actions, and an attitude of the *heart,* something rooted in the deepest part of the being. These perspectives represent a considerable progress in the spiritual consciousness of the nation — a movement from ritual to ethics,
a road to the discovery of the primacy of interiority. They pre-
pare the way slowly but surely for the teaching of Jesus.

In what did the liturgy of the Jerusalem Temple consist?
Believers expressed their relationship to the Lord by singing
psalms, by processions and blessings, but above all by offering *sacrifices.* Since the word "sacrifice" has very different connotations in our language today, we need to stop for a moment to try and understand the authentic meaning of this
notion in the Bible, thus avoiding unnecessary and useless
arguments.

Today, the expression "to make a sacrifice" has taken on
moralistic and negative overtones; it essentially means "to do
something one would rather not do out of a sense of duty."
In the ancient world, a sacrifice was first of all an offering, a
gift given to the deity. At harvest time, for example, the farmer
would offer God the firstfruits of the soil as a sign of grateful-
ness (Dt 26:1-11). Such gifts were also given to ask for forgiveness, or to mark a person's reintegration into the ordinary life
of society after an interruption. In general, to express this act
of offering a gift to the invisible God, an animal or plant was
brought to the holy place and handed over to the priest, who

often burned it. In this way he expressed that the object in question, penetrated and transformed by the fire of holiness, passed over into the divine realm; the smoke that rose up to heaven reinforced this symbolism. There were other kinds of sacrifices and other ways of offering them, but in the ancient world, a sacrifice was essentially a gift given to God and, in Israel, this was not a sad event but rather a joyful one (cf. Ps 66:13-15). When we offer a present to a particularly close friend, we consider neither the cost nor the inconvenience but rather the pleasure it will provide someone we love. Similarly, for God's people, a sacrifice expressed and reinforced their sense of belonging to the Lord who had called them into a fellowship with himself.

It is true that the Bible also contains a critique of the sacrificial system, generally emanating from prophetic circles (cf., e.g., Hos 6:6; Am 4:4-5; 5:21-25; Is 1:11-17; Ps 51:16-17). But if we look more closely, we realize that the criticism is not directed against sacrifices as such but against a hypocritical or magical attitude that placed the accent solely on fulfilling an outward rite while essential dispositions and actions were neglected.

There is another institution by means of which the people of the Bible expressed their identity as a holy nation: the *Sabbath*. In Israel, this institution has impressive credentials: it is rooted in an act of God during the creation of the universe. This is, incidentally, the first time we encounter the word "holy" in the Scriptures:

> By the seventh day God had finished the work he had been doing; so on the seventh day he rested from all his work. And God blessed the seventh day and made it holy, because on it he rested from all the work of creating that he had done.   (Gn 2:2-3)

As a result, believers must hold the seventh day different from all the others:

> The Lord said to Moses, "Say to the Israelites, 'You must
> observe my Sabbaths. This will be a sign between me and
> you for the generations to come, so that you may know
> that I am the Lord, who makes you holy. Observe the
> Sabbath, because it is holy to you.'" (Ex 31:12-14a; cf.
> Ex 20:8-11; Dt 5:12-15; Ezk 20:12)

A holy day, the Sabbath is not under the control of human beings. It is a day when people give up all self-interested
behavior in order to open themselves to God's holiness. By
ceasing their ordinary activity one day a week, believers show
that the meaning of their lives is not found in themselves. It
comes from elsewhere, as a gift they receive from God. They
recognize that they cannot master or encompass the whole of
time; a limit is set to their autonomy. The Sabbath is thus a
sign, for themselves as well as for others, of the one thing that
matters, a kind of foreshadowing of a universe entirely suffused
with the knowledge of God. Even if most disciples of Christ
no longer observe the seventh day of the week as do the Jews,
we are not dispensed from the necessity of periodically stopping the routine of daily life, which can become so all-engross-
ing, to re-center our lives on God and to become aware of the
ground of our being.

Questions for Reflection

1. Israel's prayer was expressed pre-eminently in the collection of liturgical songs called the Book of Psalms. Read
Psalms 130 and 131. What do they tell us about the atti-

tudes required of believers in order to enter into an authentic relationship with the Lord?

2. Can we rediscover for our own lives the genuine motivation behind biblical sacrifices? What can we give to God? How can we express this gift by concrete acts?

3. The institution of the Sabbath is a way of placing in the very midst of daily life a sign of the one thing that matters most. Is it possible to create in our lives spaces where we stop to rediscover God's holiness?

4. Read Numbers 20:1-13. Why, according to the author, is the miracle of water from the rock a manifestation of divine holiness (v. 13)? Does this text help us understand how human beings can "profane the Name of the Lord" (see vv. 3-5, 12)?

Mary:
The Call
as Gift

On the threshold of the Gospel of Jesus Christ, let us pause to summarize what we have discovered. We began by considering holiness as an *experience* that a human being can have, an encounter with a mysterious reality that pulls people out of their habits and routines and gives them a glimpse of another world beyond the banality of their everyday lives, a world that is simultaneously attractive and frightening. Then we noticed that, in the Bible, the experience of holiness gradually unveils its personal face: it is essentially an encounter with the God who is a "consuming fire" (Dt 4:24; Heb 12:29). And this God, far from jealously conserving his holiness for himself, aspires to communicate it. The biblical God is a God who speaks, a God who calls.

The Bible thus reveals to us a God who, down through the ages, comes to meet human beings, to call them to a fullness of life and happiness in a relationship with himself. God calls them by their *name,* in other words, in this relationship they will discover their true identity, the reason for which they were created. This relationship with the God who calls is fundamentally an open one; those touched by God transmit holiness to others by a kind of contagion, a snowball effect. The call of the faithful God thus creates a history, an ongoing continuity in time.

An important moment arrives when God creates, out of a collection of men and women on the edges of mainstream society, a holy nation, a people who are called to be, by their existence, a living sign of the divine holiness. The life of Israel, centered on the Torah of Moses, in other words the story of God's gracious call and the commands which will permit the nation to live in harmony with that call, is an attempt to incarnate holiness in the midst of human history. And this attempt is lived out under the sign of solidarity, since the call of each person finds its meaning only in the context of a community life, the life of God's people.

If the God of the Bible is, in the final analysis, a God who calls, who looks for a reciprocal relationship, it follows that the free response of the one called is an integral part of God's activity. But experience tells us that this response does not come naturally to human beings. Left to themselves, people tend instead to look for an escape, to find ways to avoid facing the call. The whole of the biblical epic can be read on the basis of this observation. God keeps on clarifying his call, removing the excuses that human beings continue to set up between themselves and the Word, until one day he finds the desired response. And then something new can happen. We witness the Covenant renewed from beginning to end.

There is a New Testament story that deals explicitly with this transition, showing how the Covenant between God and creation, traced out over the course of long centuries, is finally brought to fulfillment. This story is the well-known account of the Annunciation, the angel's announcement to Mary (Lk 1:26-38). Reading it in parallel with the story of Moses at the burning bush, we can identify both continuity and innovation. By the intermediary of his messenger, the angel Gabriel, God comes to a human being, an apparently ordinary girl living in a small town in Galilee, Mary from Nazareth. Just as for her ancestor Moses, the encounter with the world of the divine disrupts her life and causes perplexity, not to say "fear" (Lk 1:29-30; cf. 1:12). But here the accent is placed on the words spoken ("...what kind of greeting this was," 1:29); the angel comes to speak to her, to enter into a dialogue. And this dialogue contains in fact a kind of hidden call disguised as an announcement of what will happen: not "do this" but "you will do this." It is as if God is so sure of the response of his partner that he already includes it in his call.

At the beginning of this meeting, just where we would expect the divine messenger to call Mary by her name, we find these words: "Rejoice, O highly favored one, the Lord is with you" (Lk 1:28). Upon closer inspection, we discover that in fact Mary has received a new name from God. The expression translated by "you who are highly favored" or "full of grace" is a single Greek word, *kecharitômenê*, which is to be understood in this context as a title, a name. A very difficult word to translate, as can be seen by comparing different versions of the Bible, this passive perfect participle of the verb *charitoô*, "to show favor, fill with blessings" means something like "the one in whom God's grace is already fully present and at work." With respect to Moses, then, there is an important step forward: God's call is seen at the same time, and above all, as a *gift*, the gift of a Presence.

A moment later, confronted by Mary's perplexity about "how will this be?," the angel explains what this gift and this presence consist in:

> The Holy Spirit will come upon you,
> and the power of the Most High will overshadow you;
> therefore the holy one to be born in you will be called
> the Son of God.   (Lk 1:35)

The gift is nothing less than that of the divine Holiness itself, God's Breath of life, the Holy Spirit. Here we find another great advance in God's self-revelation. For Moses before the burning bush, holiness was still a reality exterior to himself. It is true that, in Israel of old, holiness was at times an inward reality in the life of the nation. God's glory filled the itinerant Shrine during the Exodus (Ex 40:34-35), and later on the great Temple of Jerusalem (1 K 8:10-12); Moses' face was radiant when he came down from Mount Sinai (Ex 34:29-35; cf. 2 Cor 3:12-18); on the eve of the Babylonian captivity, the Spirit fell upon one of the prophets (Ezk 2:2; 11:5). And Israel is called to be a holy nation who bears witness to God's holiness by observing the commandments. Although God's great gift, the Torah, remains wedded to an outward expression, words on a page, there are glimpses of greater intimacy and interiority (Dt 30:11-14; cf. Jr 31:31-34; Ezk 36:27). But here this inward presence is a key aspect of the story: the fire of holiness, the divine *Shekhinah*,[1] remains upon Mary to fulfill the promise and leads to the birth of a "holy one" who is "Son of God" (Lk 1:35). Holiness does not simply fall from the sky

---

[1] In the later Jewish tradition this word, which comes from the root *škk*, "to dwell," refers to God's presence in the world, often in the form of light, that always accompanies the people during their exile.

like a meteorite, nor is it acquired by the mere imitation of an exterior model. It *incarnates* itself, in other words it appears on the surface of history as the culmination of a long process of gestation.

The account of the angel's announcement to Mary thus emphasizes strongly God's initiative and activity. It is God who comes, announces, gives and brings about. It might seem that, as a consequence, that there is no longer any need for a response, that to God's activity corresponds human passivity. Paradoxically, exactly the opposite is true. More than ever, everything depends upon the free response of the one who receives the announcement. This response appears clearly at the end of the story:

> I am the Lord's servant; let it happen to me according to your words. (Lk 1:38)

The text also informs us about the kind of response dear to God's heart. Mary is called not to undertake this or that activity, but to *consent* to what God intends to accomplish in and through her. Consequently the emptiness that characterizes her, her insignificance in the eyes of the world (*tapeinōsis*, Lk 1:48), far from being an obstacle to the realization of her vocation, represents the "virgin" ground where God can walk unhampered (cf. Gn 3:8). By her yes to what the Lord proposes to do in a relationship with her, Mary enables God to be present in the midst of human history in a totally new way.

Questions for Reflection

In the Magnificat (Lk 1:46-55), the song that springs from her lips after meeting the angel, Mary reveals the heart of her vocation and the secret of her greatness.

1. How can a human being "exalt" or "magnify" the Lord (v. 46); does God lack something that needs to be added?
2. Why does Mary celebrate her smallness? Does her intuition help us to see our own lives — our gifts and our limits — in a new way?
3. Where do we see around us signs of the God who "scatters the proud-hearted and lifts up the lowly"?
4. According to this song, how does God show the holiness of his being (of his "Name")?

The Holy One From God

8 Working intimately with and through the people he formed and chose, with untiring patience, God prepares human hearts to respond to his call and to understand that this call is one with the gift of divine holiness. It is with unerring instinct, then, that an age-old Christian prayer compares the virginity of Mary to Moses' bush which burns without being consumed.[1] By her response which is pure receptivity, the welcoming into her existence of the sanctifying presence of God, Mary enables holiness henceforth to be fully integrated into the life of the human race. The new beginning is therefore that of the progression of holiness from within the human condition, starting from Jesus Christ, "born of a woman, born subject to the Law in order to redeem those subject to the Law..." (Gal 4:4-5).

But what is exactly the relationship between the life of this Jesus who is at the center of the Christian faith and

---

[1]   *Rubum qui viderat Moyses incombustum, conservatam agnovimus tuam laudabilem virginitatem: Dei Genitrix, intercede pro nobis* (Antiphon for the Octave of the Nativity).

all that went before him, notably in what concerns holiness? A key to answer this question is found in a story at the very end of the Gospel according to Saint Luke (24:13ff.). On the third day after the death of Jesus, two of his disciples are walking to the town of Emmaus. Christ, risen from the dead, walks alongside them but they do not recognize him. They are familiar with his entire career, including the strange rumor that he is still alive, but they are nevertheless overcome with grief. Then, at the end, during a meal they share with their unknown companion, their eyes open. Looking back, they say to one another, "Were not our hearts on fire within us while he spoke to us on the road and explained the Scriptures?" (Lk 24:32). And a few verses later, Luke tell us, "[The Risen Christ] opened their minds to understand the Scriptures" (Lk 24:45).

In other words Jesus reveals, above all by his resurrection, the deepest significance of all that God has tried to communicate to human beings in the course of their history. In Christ Jesus, the God who speaks becomes totally "Word" (cf. Jn 1:1). Christ recapitulates this communication which until then was fragmentary, disclosing its unity and all its dimensions (cf. Heb 1:1-2); he finally reveals God's deepest secret (Col 1:26-27). And he reveals it not as an abstraction but as a living reality, able to transform creatures in their entirety.

Applied to our topic, this affirmation means that it is above all in his "passover" from death to life in God that Jesus Christ unveils to us the deepest significance of holiness and communicates it to us in full. Put another way, the life, death and resurrection of Jesus provide the consummate answer to that "question" represented by the experience of holiness, and to which the previous history of the people of Israel offered some partial replies. Now we can undertake a brief reading of the Gospel with this question in mind: how does Jesus, by his life, help us understand in what the fire of God's holiness consists?

On the threshold of the Gospel we encounter a man called John, known as "The Baptizer." In the guise of a prophet of a bygone era, he calls the people to return to the roots of their existence. And he announces the coming of someone else:

> I am baptizing you with water to mark a change of heart. But the one coming after me is stronger than I am; I am not worthy to remove his sandals. He will baptize you with the Holy Spirit and with fire.   (Mt 3:11)

By means of this "stronger one" who is on the way, the fire of God's holiness will descend once and for all upon the earth. From then on, holiness will not be an experience reserved to just a few individuals, to a Moses or an Isaiah, nor even the privilege of a single nation. In the person of God's Holy Spirit, it will set the whole world on fire. It will transfigure the universe.

Then Jesus comes on the scene, and a detached observer could not fail to be struck by the gap between the extravagant language of the Baptizer and the ordinary appearance of the person about whom he had spoken. For Jesus comes as a humble man, whose first act is to ask John to baptize *him*. Far from accomplishing spectacular deeds in order to call down the fire of holiness upon the earth, Jesus begins his mission by an act of solidarity with humanity searching for God and in need of forgiveness. Here we perceive a central aspect of the Gospel: when God comes to meet his creatures, his coming surprises by its discretion, satisfying the aspirations of human beings in a way that is as unexpected as it is finally effective. The prophet Elijah had already glimpsed this reality centuries earlier when he understood that God was not in the hurricane, the earthquake or the fire, but rather in "a whisper of silence" (1 K 19:11-12).

The story of Jesus' baptism has points in common with the experience of Moses and of Mary. It is true that here, even less than for Mary, it is not essentially the account of a call. It could best be described as the eruption into the midst of the human condition of what was previously hidden. As in the case of Mary, we see the presence of the Spirit, God's holiness, fall upon Jesus:

> And at once, coming up out of the water, he saw the heavens open and the Spirit descend upon him like a dove...   (Mk 1:10)

Immediately afterwards, God calls Jesus by his new Name:

> ... and a voice came from the heavens: You are my beloved Son, on you my favor rests.   (Mk 1:11; cf. 9:7)

"You are my Son, the fruit of my love." The new Name revealed to Jesus at his baptism is thus "Son of God."[2] This is a rather unusual name. Although every human being is the son or daughter of two other persons, none of us could claim as their true name, in other words as their identity, "Son of Mrs. Smith" or "daughter of Mr. Jones." Our parents naturally contribute in important ways to the formation of our identity, but it would be an alienation to define ourselves entirely with re-

---

[2] That this expression "Son of God" should be understood as a name is even true from the point of view of the history of the text. It comes from Psalm 2:7, a royal psalm in which the new king, like the sovereigns of Egypt, receives a "throne name" when he begins his reign. Cf. Isaiah 9:5 (6). See H.-J. Kraus, *Theology of the Psalms* (London: SPCK/Minneapolis: Augsburg Publishing House, 1986), p. 113.

spect to them. Human parenthood is relative; our parents transmit a life they have received in their turn from elsewhere. They are not the source (cf. Eph 3:14-15).

Reflecting on this name of Jesus, we can better understand how he is unique. Being "God's Son" is not for him one quality among many, one sentence in a long curriculum vitae. His identity is totally determined by the fact that he is "the Son"; in other words, Jesus defines himself uniquely through a relationship with the one he calls "Abba" (cf. Mk 14:36). There is nothing that remains outside this relation, no walled-off corner that he guards jealously for himself and that he views as his true self. If Jesus is complete openness to God, it necessarily follows from this that his existence reveals fully the identity of his Abba. Jesus states this himself in a prayer spoken at a later point in his ministry:

> Everything has been handed over to me by my Father,
> and no one knows the Son but the Father;
> and no one knows the Father but the Son
> and whoever the Son wishes to reveal him to.
>   (Mt 11:27)

Since he is the one who *is*, and whose existence has meaning, solely through his relationship with God, Jesus reveals that this God is the Source of all — the Source of life and the Source of meaning. In other words, God is essentially "Abba" or, as Saint John puts it in a different language: "God is Love" (1 Jn 4:8,16). Because his whole life is an absolutely faithful reflection of God's life, Jesus is able to enlighten us better than anyone else concerning the meaning of divine holiness.

At the same time, we should not forget that Jesus was not the only member of the Jewish nation to offer a vision of holiness. At the beginning of the common era all Jews were in agreement that, to be faithful to God, it was necessary to be holy. But how? Some gave a radical reply to this question: holiness required a complete break with a world they considered impure. This logic led them to leave the society of the time and settle on the banks of the Dead Sea in what could almost be considered a monastic community. They were members of the Essene movement, with which John the Baptist may have had some connection. Others practiced their separation while still remaining members of society by undertaking distinctive and demanding religious practices: this was the party of the Pharisees, a very influential lay movement at the time of Jesus, particularly strong outside the large urban centers. Thus the image of holiness manifested in the life and teaching of Jesus differed implicitly from other ways of understanding holiness current at that time.[3]

Let us now continue our reading of the Gospel according to Saint Mark, the first chapters of which present a whole catechesis on the theme of holiness, a progressive disclosing of its content. After his baptism, his temptations and the first proclamation of the "good news" (Mk 1:1-15), Jesus begins his activity on the banks of the Lake of Galilee. There he sees four fishermen at work. He invites these ordinary men to accompany him, and at once they leave work, family and friends to join him (Mk 1:16-20). From the start, then, Mark shows us that in this itinerant preacher there is something able to spark a radical change of lifestyle in people by means of a simple encounter, without any pressure at all being exercised. Jesus' presence attracts to such an extent that the rest of life appears

---

[3] For a reading of the Gospel in terms of different "programs" of holiness in confrontation with one another see Marcus J. Borg, *Conflict, Holiness and Politics in the Teachings of Jesus* (New York/Toronto: The Edwin Mellon Press, 1984).

insipid by comparison. He is the bearer of an absolute such that, by his mere arrival on the scene, everything is reoriented around him. Here we have a kind of preliminary definition of holiness that emerges from the first pages of the Gospel.

In the following story (Mk 1:21-28), this "power of attraction" of Jesus takes on a more precise shape. Listening to his words in the synagogue of Capharnaum, the hearers "were all so astonished that they asked one another: 'What is this? A new teaching, given with authority!'" (1:27). This mixture of fascination and fright reminds us of Moses' reaction in front of the burning bush. Jesus' words contain within them a force able to touch people's hearts and turn things upside down. The Gospel-writer emphasizes this fact by mentioning that in the synagogue a man "possessed by an unclean spirit" is present (1:23), someone at the opposite extreme from God's holiness. The same words by which Jesus communicates his teaching sends the unclean spirit away and restores the possessed man to health. Ironically, that spirit reveals the key that enables us to understand the story: "You have come to destroy us. I know who you are: the Holy One from God" (1:24; cf. Lk 1:35). God's holiness manifests itself in Jesus as a life-giving power able to vanquish the forces of evil.

A little later, another healing accomplished by Jesus shows this combat in even more dramatic fashion. A leper comes to Jesus to be cured (Mk 1:40-45). In biblical times, leprosy was viewed as a particularly malignant disease. A typically modern mentality, which separates the different domains of life, for example the material and the spiritual, into airtight compartments, does not make it easy for us to understand the attitude of Jesus' contemporaries in the face of this affliction. They for their part made no distinction between the fear of catching a contagious disease and horror at an evil power that made people religiously unclean. They did not separate an attack against wholeness from one against holiness. In any event, the consequences were the same: the leper had to be excluded from the company of others, since his presence was a danger to the life of society. When that unfortunate man "came up" to Jesus, therefore, his act was an implicit threat, which could with good reason be considered an act of aggression.

Set in this context, Jesus' response is extremely significant. "Jesus put out his hand and touched him." Far from fleeing the powers of evil, the Holy One from God (cf. 1:24) goes toward those they hold in bondage and seeks to make contact. And instead of Jesus being made unclean, the "contamination" goes in the other direction and the sick man is restored to health: "At once the leprosy left him and he became clean" (1:42). Jesus is shown to be the "stronger one," able to overcome the forces of evil which were apparently so formidable (cf. Mt 3:11; Lk 11:21-22). In him, God's holiness is not a treasure to be protected but a force of healing that goes out to conquer the world.

The following episode (Mk 2:1-12) shows that the healing of the body is in fact the sign of something much deeper. A paralyzed man is brought to Jesus, and instead of the expected words of healing, Jesus says, "My child, your sins are forgiven." Only later comes the invitation: "Get up and walk!" Here it becomes clear that God's holiness goes down to the very roots of evil; it is capable of purifying the depths of our being. This inner healing, called the forgiveness of sins, offers to people bowed down under the weight of their faults a new beginning in a relationship with God: "Get up and walk!"

Next, the Gospel-writer shows us the social consequences of this energy of forgiveness set loose by Jesus (Mk 2:13-17). Jesus approaches a tax-collector, a member of a group of people particularly despised for religious, political and social reasons, and invites him to be one of his intimates. Then he enters his home to eat a meal — an unmistakable sign of fellowship at that time — with "sinners." Here holiness is shown as a force for reconciliation and communion. It impels Jesus to go towards those who are apparently far from God, so that they can enter a new relationship with the Lord, which will have as a consequence the establishment of new relationships among human beings.

It should be obvious at this point that holiness as Jesus reveals it runs counter to a good number of convictions deeply rooted in Israel. Those for whom the quest for holiness was identical with a careful separation from all that was "impure" would not fail to be shocked by the behavior of Jesus (cf. Mk 2:16). "That man welcomes sinners and eats with them! ... If that man were a prophet, he would know what kind of woman is touching him. ... He has gone to stay at the home of a sinner!" (Lk 15:2; 7:39; 19:7). Jesus for his part obeys a quite different logic. Like a doctor, he looks for people who are most in need and goes to meet them, to share with them a love able to make possible a new beginning.

In the Gospels, therefore, what Jesus or his disciples do often leads to arguments with those who hold positions of authority in the nation of Israel. And whether the word is spoken or not, these controversies inevitably have to do with an understanding of what holiness is. A particularly significant example is the complete lack of agreement concerning the institution of the Sabbath, so important in post-exilic Judaism. There, two radically incompatible visions clash and, as a result, it is no surprise that Jesus' attitude regarding the Sabbath became one of the principal motives for attacking him (Mk 3:6; Jn 5:16; 7:23; 9:16). For Jesus, the fact of healing someone on that holy day was a manifestation of the true meaning of holiness and thus particularly appropriate, whereas for his opponents, who saw things only from the outside, it was a form of work and thus forbidden by the Law (Mk 3:1-6). Similarly, for the Pharisees, to call Jesus "a friend of sinners" (Mt 11:19) was a way of disqualifying him; for Jesus, however, it corresponded well to the program he was attempting to put into practice. The same facts receive diametrically different interpretations, which in the final analysis witness to a divergence with regard to a basic attitude towards the whole of life.

Questions for Reflection

1. Read Luke 10:30-37. In this story there are two ways of understanding holiness. What are they? Why does Jesus tell this story; what does he want us to understand?
2. Read Matthew 12:1-14. To understand fully the significance of these stories, we must realize that Jesus does not intend to neglect observance of the Sabbath but rather is trying to reveal its true meaning. How does Jesus help us understand here what holiness is?

Happy the Pure in Heart

9 There is another aspect of holiness, present in embryo in the Hebrew Scriptures, which is at the heart of Jesus' revelation of this reality. This aspect becomes explicit in the Beatitudes (Mt 5:1-12), a key text which the evangelist Matthew places at the head of the great "program" we know as the Sermon on the Mount. It is found in the sixth beatitude: "Happy the pure in heart: they shall see God" (Mt 5:8; cf. Heb 12:14). These words open up essential perspectives for our investigation.

Let us first examine the promise at the end of the phrase. In the Hebrew Scriptures, the expression "to see God" refers to the act of being admitted into the Lord's presence, notably in the Temple of Jerusalem (Dt 31:11; Ps 42:2). We have see that the Law of Moses attempted to establish conditions for the access of the faithful to the holy place. Ritual purity, which basically consists in satisfying these conditions, is required in order to "serve before God's face," to take part in the worship of the holy people. In the sixth beatitude, then, Jesus takes up the intuition of the author of Psalm 24: to be qualified to come into contact with the Holy One, what matters is above all an attitude of the heart (cf. Ps 24:4). It can therefore be said that, for Jesus, holiness is a reality rooted above all in the human heart.

To avoid misunderstandings, it is essential to recall the precise meaning of the word "heart" in the Bible. Whereas today the heart stands primarily for the feelings, the emotions, in the Bible it refers to a more central and more inclusive reality. The heart is the core of a person, the point of convergence where all the human faculties come together. It is the seat of reflection as well as of decision. When we ask ourselves questions such as "Why am I here on earth? What is the meaning of my life? What does God want from me?" that is the biblical heart speaking. And it is there, according to Jesus, that holiness takes root and is, so to speak, in its natural element.

This way of looking at human beings is so essential for Jesus that he reacts vehemently when it is called into question. By nature so "gentle and humble of heart" (Mt 11:29), he does not hesitate to raise his voice when the essential is at stake:

> Woe to you, scribes and Pharisees, you hypocrites! You clean the outside of cups and plates, while inside they are full of greed and self-indulgence. Blind Pharisee, first clean the inside of the cup, so that the outside too will become clean. Woe to you, scribes and Pharisees, you hypocrites! You are like whitewashed graves, which are pleasant to look at on the outside but within are full of dead bones and all kinds of corruption. This is the case for you, too: outwardly you look like upright persons, but inside you are filled with hypocrisy and lawlessness.   (Mt 23:25-28)

Jesus denounces a reduction of purity to outward behavior and a dangerous split between the outside and the inside of a human being that results from this. In all our modern translations of the Bible, the term "hypocrisy" is used to indicate this split. Unfortunately, this word as we use it today in common parlance does not correspond exactly to the attitude criticized by Jesus. For us, hypocrisy is basically a lack of sincerity, while Jesus is trying to warn us about an inability or a refusal to see the link between what is in our hearts and how we act. In other words, even were we to assume that most of the Pharisees were indeed sincere in believing that what mattered was only outward behavior, that would not modify Jesus' criticism of them. They were not "hypocrites" because they did not act according to their convictions (some, of course, may *also* have been hypocrites in this sense), but precisely because they were led astray by their convictions and did not recognize the need for a unification of their personality starting from the heart. In this respect they are close to the *dipsychoi* criticized by Saint James (Jm 1:8; 4:8), "two-souled" individuals, split personalities who do not see the fissure that is in them.

Jesus gives a similar teaching, likewise expressed in negative fashion, in the following words where his pressing concern to be understood is manifest:

> And once again calling the crowd around him, he said to them: Listen to me, all of you, and get this into your head! There is nothing outside a person that can make him unclean by entering him. No, what comes *out* of a person is what makes that person unclean. (...) For it is from within, from a person's heart, that evil designs come forth: sexual immorality, thievery, murder (...). All these evil things come out of a person and make that person unclean. (Mk 7:14-15, 21-23)

In the days of Jesus, it was necessary to make people realize that in God's eyes, an act in itself is less important than
its source within the person. Today, in the Western world
marked by centuries of rampant individualism and influenced
by a so-called "depth psychology" which in fact often only deals
with the surface levels of personality, the danger comes from
a different direction. It lies in confusing the biblical heart with
psychological realities and putting undue emphasis on intro-
spection. A complicity between psychology and faith that is too
one-sided risks leading to new separations. In this respect we
should remember that the Semitic mentality does not separate the parts of the being but sees them as symbols of the
whole. The biblical heart is the *whole* person seen from the
viewpoint of his or her deepest point, the capacity to enter into
a relationship with God.[1]

To put it more concretely, many of our contemporaries
would understand Jesus' words concerning the heart in the
following way: "What counts is my basic intention. If I have
good intentions, the rest is of little import." They do not realize that this interpretation simply turns the Pharisees' error
on its head. The latter excluded the intention; the former
exclude the act. Jesus, for his part, emphasizes the unity between the two, though he does accord a priority to the inner
dimension since it is closer to the source. On another occa-

---

[1] Some see the work of Martin Luther as unwittingly marking this shift, especially in his interpretation of Saint Paul. Luther read Paul, via Augustine,
in function of a new historical context in which the Apostle's reflections
on the Torah of Moses and the place of non-Jews in God's plan were rein-
terpreted as a response to the existential anguish of the individual conscience searching for the certainty of salvation. In this respect see the illuminating article of the Lutheran bishop Krister Stendahl, "The Apostle Paul
and the Introspective Conscience of the West," reprinted in his work *Paul
Among Jews and Gentiles* (Philadelphia: Fortress Press, 1976).

sion, Jesus explains this unity by an image that is quite accessible:

> No good tree produces rotten fruit, nor does a rotten tree produce good fruit. Every tree is known by the fruit it produces. You do not pick figs from a thornbush, nor gather grapes on briers. A good person, from the good treasure of his heart, brings forth what is good, and an evil person, from the evil within him, brings forth evil. The mouth speaks when the heart overflows.
>
> (Lk 6:43-45)

The essential takes place within a person but is inevitably translated into outward acts. Holiness dwells in the heart, but radiates outward from there to transform all of life. The most important question, then, is not "How can I perform good acts?" but rather "How can I acquire a pure heart?", one which will necessarily lead to outward acts of goodness. And would any of us with a minimum of self-knowledge claim to possess a perfectly pure heart?

Where, then, does purity of heart come from? How can it be acquired? First of all, a person cannot acquire it by his or her own acts. This is because, on the one hand, no one is master of their own heart (cf. Jr 17:9-10), and on the other hand, the only detergent able to cleanse the heart is the fire of God's holiness (cf. Ml 3:1-4). Centuries before Christ, a believer had already realized this when he prayed: "Create in me a pure heart, O God" (Ps 51:10). He saw the cleansing of his heart as an act of creation which consequently only the Creator could accomplish. In his turn Jesus, in an allegory where he takes up again the image of a plant — here a vine — destined to bear fruit, explains:

> I am the true vine and my Father is the vine-grower (…).
> He cleanses every fruit-bearing branch so that it may
> bear even more. Already you are clean through the word
> which I have spoken to you.   (Jn 15:1-3)

Jesus explains to his disciples that "the words of eternal life" (cf. Jn 6:68) which he communicates to them initiate a kind of permanent process of purification which leads them to bear more and more fruit. Having a pure heart is thus not a fixed state, but rather means participating in a process which begins with an act of welcoming God's holiness and continues by letting this holiness consume one after another all the resistances we oppose to God's activity. "Whoever has this hope in them becomes pure just as [Christ] is pure" (1 Jn 3:3). On the human side, the important thing is to open our hearts ("You believe in God, believe also in me," Jn 14:1) and to remain faithful to this basic attitude ("remain in me just as I remain in you," Jn 15:4), in other words to welcome God's word (Jn 12:48) and to keep it (Jn 14:23; cf. 8:31) so that it can permeate the whole of our existence *(chôreo,* Jn 8:37). The rest will come as an unexpected bonus: "Whoever remains in me and I in them, that person will bear much fruit" (Jn 15:5).

Saint Paul in turn expresses the same reality of transformation by using the image of light:

> The God who said: *Let light shine in the darkness,* is the
> one who has shined in our hearts to reveal the knowl-
> edge of God's glory shining on the face of Christ.
> (2 Cor 4:6)

And this radiance of God's holiness ("glory") in our hearts gradually transforms them so that they may be more and more in the image of Christ:

And all of us who, with our faces uncovered, reflect the
Lord's glory as in a mirror, are transformed into that
same image, with ever-increasing glory, in conformity
with the activity of the Lord who is Spirit. (2 Cor 3:18)

Questions for Reflection

1. Read Matthew 6:19-21. What is my treasure? How can I
   "store up treasures in heaven"?
2. "Choosing Christ means walking on one road, not two
   at the same time." What do these words mean concretely
   for my life?
3. How does the attitude of Mary who "kept everything,
   meditating on it in her heart" (Lk 2:19, 51) offer us an
   approach to Christian holiness?
4. Saint James advises the *dipsychoi* (double-souled people)
   to "purify their hearts" (Jm 4:8). How does this text help
   us understand the link between purity or holiness and
   inner unity? What does it tell us about the roots of Christian simplicity?

Emptiness and Fullness

10 "An energy came out of him and healed them all" (Lk 6:19). By his words and his acts, Jesus takes his place in the main line of biblical revelation. God's holiness at work in him, far from being a movement of separation, is a dynamic reality that impels him towards others. Still more, it is a power that heals body and soul, that brings the fullness of life to those who are in need. On a spiritual level, this healing bears the name of forgiveness, of reconciliation. Holiness is thus shown to be an energy that creates communion, a communion with God which has as its inevitable consequence a communion among human beings.

The same result can be attained by another road. Jesus takes a stand against any fragmenting of human life, any reduction of religion to acts which can be accomplished mechanically and do not implicate the entire being. He constantly places the accent on what the Bible calls the heart, the unifying center of the individual. That is where holiness is rooted, and from there it sets out to transform the whole of life, like a tree which bears its fruit at the appropriate time. In his teaching and his actions, therefore, Jesus attempts above all to reach the heart of his listeners in order to awaken it and to bring about a *metanoia*,[1] a radical change of outlook. Jesus thus shows holiness to be fundamentally a *personal* reality. In the Gospel, what might appear from the outside as an anonymous force or energy is revealed, in the final analysis, to be the consequence of a personal encounter. Holiness finds its source and its goal in such an encounter, another name for communion.

In thus revealing, by word and deed, the meaning of holiness, Jesus simply expresses the reality of his being. We have seen that, at his baptism, he receives a unique name: he is God's beloved Son, the one whose entire being is defined by a relationship of love, by a communion with the One he calls "Abba." Of all the Gospels, it is the Gospel according to Saint John that best expresses this unique identity of Jesus. If the Synoptic Gospels allow us to follow the itinerant preacher from Nazareth step by step until finally we recognize in him "the Messiah, the Son of the living God" (Mt 16:16), John fixes our gaze from the very beginning upon the person of Jesus, the only one who reveals the fullness of God (Jn 1:18; 14:6), the Source of eternal life for the world (Jn 3:16; 17:2).

Already in the titles it employs, the Fourth Gospel shows its specific character. In John's Gospel, Jesus does not call himself "the Son of God" but simply "the Son," as if to emphasize that this is not a mere description but a true Name. And he uses two chief names for God, both of which express a relationship: "the Father" and "the One who sent me." Christ does

---

[1] *Metanoia*: a Greek word often translated by "repentance" or "conversion" but which signifies above all a transformation of one's way of thinking and acting, a reorientation of one's entire being as a result of an encounter with the living God. Cf. Mark 1:15.

not contemplate God as an isolated and self-sufficient being, who only subsequently looks outward. No, each time Jesus evokes the mystery of God, Being-in-relation, he is led by the very same movement to go deeper into his own mystery. If there is a Father, there must be a Son, and if God is the One who sends, then someone must be sent.

Towards the end of the Fourth Gospel, in the final prayer to his Father, Jesus reveals the full reality of this being-in-relation, in a kind of consummate definition of communion:

> All that is mine is yours, and yours mine.
> (Jn 17:10; cf. 10:30; 14:11)

At this point we can even ask ourselves whether the term "relationship" is applicable to this total sharing of life that we have indicated by the word communion, where the two partners are not only situated face-to-face, but each is also within the other. In any event, the words we use are not the important thing as long as we grasp the underlying reality as accurately as possible. Let us now look at some of the aspects of this communion in which the existence of Jesus is rooted, accessible through the words he speaks throughout John's Gospel:

> The Father loves the Son
> and has given all things into his hand....
> The Son can do nothing by himself
> that he does not see the Father doing;
> for whatever that one does
> the Son does too in the same way.
> For the Father loves the Son
> and shows him everything he does....
> I can do nothing by myself...
> because I do not seek my own will

> but the will of the One who sent me....
> Don't you believe
> that I am in the Father and the Father is in me?
> The words that I speak to you,
> I do not speak them of myself;
> the Father who remains in me is doing his work.
>
> (Jn 3:35; 5:19-20,30; 14:10)

Looking more closely, we can distinguish two principal dimensions of this relationship of communion that unites the Father and the Son. At first glance they seem contradictory, but this apparent contradiction is in fact a call to go deeper.

First of all, there are texts which emphasize what we can call the *negative* aspect of the relationship. Jesus is nothing in himself (Jn 8:42); he can do nothing (5:19,30; 6:38; 8:28) and say nothing (7:16; 12:49; 14:10,24) on his own. Other passages bring out the *positive* aspect: Jesus possesses everything, because he has received everything from the Father: being (8:42; 10:36), life (5:26; 6:57), the authority to judge (5:22,27), his teaching (7:16; 8:38; 12:49-50; 14:24), and his glory (8:54; 13:31-32; cf. 5:41,44). In other words, Jesus is both totally poor and totally rich. Having nothing of his own, he has everything at his disposal, because the Father has placed all things in his hands (3:35; cf. 16:15). He is perfectly obedient,[2] because he always does what the Father wishes (8:29), and perfectly free,

---

[2] The use of the word "obedience" in the realm of faith is a delicate business, to a great extent because of ambiguities more or less consciously fostered across the ages. What could be easier for unjust authorities than to invoke the deity to justify their hegemony and to repress every manifestation of freedom? The sad conclusion of this hoax, in the spiritual history of the Western world, was the development of the myth of a dictator-god who had to be killed for human beings to reach their full maturity and freedom. For the Gospel, though, obedience has nothing to do with a slavish attitude (cf. Rom 8:15). The word must be understood in its original sense, listening and responding in trust (*ob-audire*).

because he knows that the Father always pays attention to his requests (11:42).

This accord between two attitudes that seem incompatible to us follows directly from the unique identity of Jesus, from the fact that he is the Son. By claiming to be nothing in himself and by receiving everything from the Father, Jesus expresses perfectly the truth of who he is. Far from submitting to violence, he manifests by his "self-emptying" (cf. Ph 2:6-7) the place freely given and freely accepted that is his from all eternity in the loving design *(eudokia,* "good pleasure," cf. Eph 1:5,9) of the Father. And the key that enables us to solve the riddle is love: "The Father loves the Son..." (Jn 3:35; 5:20; cf. 10:17). Jesus is the *beloved* Son (Mk 1:11; 9:7) and love alone makes possible a relationship which is not in the final analysis alienation, domination of the weaker partner by the stronger one.

In chapter 4 of John's Gospel, Jesus uses a graphic image to underline the paradox, humanly speaking, of his relationship with God. The disciples have returned from the town with provisions and want to nourish their master after his tiring journey. He replies, "I have food to eat that you know nothing about." They are perplexed, a typical attitude in this Gospel for those who have not yet acquired God's perspective on things (Jn 4:31-33). And Jesus continues:

> My food is to do the will of the One who sent me and to
> bring his work to fulfillment. (Jn 4:34)

Far from being something that oppresses him or that takes away his freedom, the Father's will is *nourishment* for Jesus, in other words something that gives him life, that makes him more himself. If he is the Son, then it is by trying to welcome freely and joyfully everything that comes to him from the Father, and to respond by putting it into practice, that he expresses his true identity. God is truly a Source of life for him (Jn 6:57); his entire existence consists in expressing a relationship of receiving and giving that is called communion.

While emphasizing in this way the close relationship between the Father and the Son, Saint John does not forget that it is a relationship characterized by holiness and thus fundamentally an open one. Intimacy goes hand in hand with being sent out to others. This is already clear from the aforementioned two names with which Jesus designates God: "the Father" and "the One who sent me." Christ is simultaneously the Word "into the Father's bosom"[3] (Jn 1:18) who "was in the beginning with God" (1:2), and the One who comes (3:31; 11:27; 12:13), the One sent from the Father (6:57; 8:42; 10:36). And the fact of being sent out on mission does not mean that he and the Father are not constantly present to one another: "...the One who sent me is with me; he did not leave me alone" (8:29; cf. 16:32).

The only Son of God, Jesus is sent into the world to give life to human beings, in other words to open to them his own relationship with the Father (Jn 1:18; 3:16-17). In his visibility at the heart of human history, he makes present a space where human beings can contemplate the invisible God (Jn 12:45; 14:9-11; cf. Col 1:15). The Son fulfills his mission by giving to human beings what the Father has given him:

> Just as the Father, who lives, has sent me
> and I live through the Father,

---

[3] This is a literal and therefore awkward translation of the Greek in order to underline the fact that Jesus is not only "at the Father's side" (NIV) but is turned toward the Father and constantly approaching him in a movement of ever-increasing intimacy. Their relationship is not at all a static one; it is pure dynamism, activity. "Fire never says, 'Enough!'" (Prov 30:16).

in the same way the one who eats me
will live through me....
I say what I say
just as the Father said it to me....
I have loved you,
just as the Father has loved me....
Just as you sent me into the world,
so have I sent them into the world.

(Jn 6:57; 12:50; 15:9; 17:18)

In other words, Jesus responds to the Father by taking
on responsibility for those whom the Father has given him.

Questions for Reflection

1. Read John 20:11-18. What keeps Mary from realizing that
   Jesus is risen? What enables her finally to recognize the
   Risen Christ? What are the consequences of this?
2. Reply to the above questions again, replacing "Mary" with
   "us."

Father, Glorify Your Name!

11 Jesus is "the Holy One from God" (Mk 1:24), the one whose existence consists in a relationship with the one he calls "Abba," a relationship of welcome and response. As "the Son," Jesus reconciles in himself perfect obedience and total freedom. His life is essentially that of a being-in-relation, a way of existing through and for Another. And he expresses his existence for that Other who is God by living for others who are human beings. His relationship with the Father is constitutive of a responsibility towards us. This identity of Jesus that we have just summarized finds its expression in all the words and actions of his life that are reported in the Gospels. But it is above all the end of his life that recapitulates this identity and expresses it fully. To understand this, we can profitably begin with these enigmatic words of Jesus:

> I have come to cast fire on the earth, and how I wish it were already burning! I have to be baptized with a baptism, and how anxious I am until it is accomplished! (Lk 12:49-50)

Earlier, the Baptizer had announced that someone more powerful would come to bring to earth the fire of God's holiness (Mt 3:11). In undertaking this mission, Jesus speaks of it as something still to come in the future, although he is already communicating the Good News of the Kingdom in word and deed. And while John had spoken of that baptism as an *activity* to be undertaken by the one who would come, Jesus describes it here as something he must submit to. What does this expression mean to him? Another text helps us answer this question. When two of his disciples ask for the most important places in God's Kingdom, Jesus replies:

> You do not know what you are asking. Can you drink
> the cup I will drink, or be baptized with the baptism I
> will undergo?   (Mk 10:38)

The cup and the baptism are obviously images that evoke the suffering and violent death which Jesus realizes lie in store for him. We can now interpret the words of Jesus in Luke 12 as a veiled announcement that it is by his passion and death, by the gift of his life to the end, that the fire of divine holiness will be kindled on the earth. Although Jesus' entire existence was an attempt to reveal and communicate God's holiness, the end of his earthly career will be the definitive revelation and the full communication of this holiness.

It is John's Gospel once again that gives us the deepest insight into a reality of faith, here by showing the essential link between the end of Jesus' life and the revelation of holiness. Since the texts that deal with this are extremely dense and allusive, however, they must be read slowly and attentively. In chapter 12, we find ourselves in Jerusalem during the Passover feast:

There were some Greeks among those who came up to
worship during the feast. So they came to Philip, who
was from Bethsaida in Galilee, and asked him, "Sir, we
want to see Jesus." Philip went and told Andrew, and
then Andrew and Philip went to tell Jesus. (Jn 12:20-22)

A few non-Jews ("Greeks") in the huge throng of pilgrims
filling Jerusalem wish to see Jesus. We are justified in wonder-
ing why the evangelist dwells so long on a detail which seems
so insignificant from a purely historical point of view. As always in such cases in the Fourth Gospel, it is a sign that the
fact possesses a profound symbolic meaning in John's eyes.

We should remember that the people of Israel had received the calling to be "a people of priests, a holy nation," in
other words a people that, by its very existence, would bear
witness to the identity of its God before the whole human race.
In fact, the Bible shows us that, most of the time, Israel did
not fill this role adequately. Instead of "making holy the Lord's
Name" by walking in God's ways, the nation more often than
not "profaned the Name" by its unfaithfulness. And yet in each
generation there were upright souls who placed their trust in
God's faithfulness. These men and women were convinced
that one day the Lord would find a way to keep his promise
by causing his holiness to shine out; it would radiate from the
holy city and be seen by all humankind. The prophets expressed this hope in glowing images:

> Arise, shine, for your light has come,
> and the glory of the Lord rises upon you.
> See, darkness covers the earth
> and thick darkness is over the peoples,
> but the Lord rises upon you
> and his glory appears over you.

> Nations will come to your light,
> and kings to the brightness of your dawn.
> Lift up your eyes and look about you:
> all assemble and come to you....
> (Is 60:1-4; cf. 2:2-4; Zc 8:20-23; 14:16)

And now, in the apparently banal fact of a handful of foreigners who want to see the prophet from Nazareth, Saint John realizes that this centuries-old longing is now becoming reality. That is why Jesus' reaction is so dramatic:

> Jesus replied, "The hour has come for the Son of man
> to be glorified."   (Jn 12:23)

When we examined the experience of the prophet Isaiah in the Temple, we defined God's glory as the radiance of his holiness (Is 6:3). One of the major themes of John's Gospel is that by the signs he accomplishes during his life, Jesus manifests this glory to those who have eyes to see it (Jn 2:11; 1:14). At the same time, all these manifestations are only partial. They point toward a *kairos*, a critical moment of full and final revelation, an event that Jesus calls "his hour" (2:4; 7:30; 8:20; cf. 7:6,8). When he sees some non-Jews come to look for him, then Jesus realizes that the time has finally come to reveal fully God's holiness in his existence.

But this manifestation, according to a "law" characteristic of divine revelation, will come about in the most unexpected way possible. And so, to help his hearers grasp what is afoot, Jesus looks for a comparison drawn from daily life:

> I tell you the truth: unless a grain of wheat falls into the
> earth and dies, it remains a single grain; but if it dies, it
> bears much fruit.   (Jn 12:24)

The "glorification" of Jesus will not come about through a movement of exaltation, by the quest for honor, prestige or power in the image of his opponents who "take their glory from one another" (Jn 5:44). The glory of the Son (his true identity and the divine holiness fully present in him) will be revealed by a movement that goes in the opposite direction — by the unconditional gift of his life, by an apparent failure which is in fact the only road to true fruitfulness. Then Jesus shows the consequences of this for human behavior, valuable for all his disciples:

> Whoever clings to their life will lose it; and whoever is not attached to their life in this world will keep it safe for eternal life.   (Jn 12:25)

The text says literally, "whoever *loves* their life... whoever *hates* their life...." Semitic languages have a hard time expressing comparisons, and tend to do so by juxtaposing opposites. Jesus clearly is not condemning a healthy self-love, nor is he preaching self-hatred. He is pointing to the question of *priorities,* asking who we place at the center of the universe, ourselves or God (and as a result all God's creatures). The alternative is either to focus on ourselves out of fear or complacency, or else to give and serve out of love.

Jesus does not desire suffering and death as an end in itself — he is "troubled" by what he sees before him (12:27) — but he is convinced that this is the only path on which he can reveal God's holiness to the world. In addition, Jesus is well aware that, like everything in his existence, this road will lead somewhere only through the collaboration of the one he calls "Abba." The gift he will make of his life is something of a far different order from an act of magic originating in a soli-

tary "omnipotence"; it is worked out in communion, expressed
in a prayer of confident trust addressed to the Father:

> Now my soul is troubled, and what shall I say? Father,
> save me from this hour! But it is for this very reason that
> I came to this hour. Father, glorify your Name! A voice
> came from the sky: "I have glorified it and I will glorify
> it yet again."   (Jn 12:27-28)

And the sign by which we can know that this prayer was
heard is the unity among human beings to which it will lead.
The full manifestation of holiness will liberate in the universe
an unprecedented energy of reconciliation:

> And once I am lifted up from the earth, I will attract all
> people to myself. He said this to signify by what kind of
> death he was destined to die.   (Jn 12:32-33)

The Synoptic Gospels show this same road towards the
full revelation of holiness in the guise of a dramatic combat.
In Gethsemane, Jesus expresses this in an intimate dialogue
with the Father:

> My Father, if it be possible, let this cup pass me by. Not
> as I wish, though, but as you wish.   (Mt 26:39)

It is essential to realize that this prayer is in no way an
expression of a fatalistic outlook, of a forced consent. Here
Jesus is at grips with the utter reality of evil; he has entered
fully into the darkness and confusion created by the refusal
of love. And precisely in this situation where he no longer has
any distance and where everything seems to point to another
meaning, or even to meaninglessness, he escapes from the
impasse by discovering and expressing once again his deep-

est identity. For him, as the Son, the road to life can only be that of trusting in his beloved Abba. As always, Jesus finds a way out by seeking the Father's will and by putting it into practice.

If we ask why Jesus had to enter fully into the reality of evil, the answer can only be this: not for himself but for us. If Jesus had never had this experience, it would be easy for us to say, "True, he was always obedient to his Father, but after all, he was God's only Son and knew full well what was going on. Things are not the same for me. So often I am lost and confused; I don't know what to do."

In the Garden of Olives, Jesus is in no way in a privileged situation. He is not a detached observer who can see and understand clearly what is happening to him. What he does is therefore of the utmost importance for us; it shows us a road that is always possible — to make an act of trust in the heart of the darkness.

But if Jesus' act is to have this value, it must be a free response, not an obligation. Here again, Saint John is the one who shows most clearly this dimension of Jesus' gift of his life:

> That is why the Father loves me, because I lay down my life in order to take it up again. No one takes it from me; I lay it down of my own volition. I have authority to lay it down, and I have authority to take it up again: this is the commandment I have received from my Father.
>
> (Jn 10:17-18)

To grasp the deepest meaning of the death of Jesus, we have to realize that he bows to no external necessity. He is acting in full conformity with his own identity as the Son of the Father. That is why he can say both "I am giving my life freely" and "this is the commandment I have received from

my Father." Once again for Jesus, as the Son, there is no contradiction between being himself ("free") and following the
will of the Father.

During his last conversation with his disciples, Jesus explains the meaning of this free gift of self from another point
of view:

> ...the Prince of this world is coming. He has no hold
> on me, but it is so that the world may know that I love
> the Father and do as the Father has commanded me.
>
> (Jn 14:30-31)

Far from being a defeat or submission to a malevolent
power, the death of Christ is described, here again, as the revelation of Jesus' identity as God's beloved Son. By consenting
to the Father's will to save all humanity (cf. 1 Tm 2:3-4), Jesus
transforms the reign of darkness into the transmission of life
and holiness.

A little later in John's Gospel, these same themes are
taken up again and developed. Chapter 17, by allowing us to
enter into the great prayer which Jesus addresses to his Father
during the Last Supper, gives us a unique perspective on the
divine life shared by Father and Son; we witness from within,
as it were, the common life of the Trinity. And here once again
our theme reappears. With the Father's help, the hour of
Jesus' death will be the complete revelation of holiness, and
will be made concrete by the gift of the fullness of life to human beings:

> Lifting his eyes to heaven, Jesus said, "Father, the hour
> has come. Glorify your Son, so that your Son may glo-
> rify you and, since you have given him authority over
> all flesh, so that he may give eternal life to all you have
> given to him."   (Jn 17:1-2)

Then Jesus explains how this collaboration between himself and the Father will come about:

> I have glorified you on earth; I have completed the work
> you gave me to do. And now, Father, glorify me in your
> presence with the glory I had in your presence before
> the world existed.   (Jn 17:4-5)

These phrases are extremely dense, and must be unpacked. First of all, Jesus is explaining that his entire life has been an attempt to make God's holiness present and visible on earth. Now, he is getting ready to crown this work by giving his life to the very end. The Greek verb *teleioô*, "to finish, fulfill," and its cognates tend to evoke in the Fourth Gospel the death of Christ, or rather the definitive gift of his life (cf. Jn 4:34; 19:28,30; 13:1). He thus turns to the Father and asks him to act in a way that will make fruitful what he, Jesus, is going to do, since once he is dead he will no longer be able to do anything to ensure the "success" of his work. From this point of view as well, Jesus has no other alternative than to trust by placing his spirit completely in the Father's hands.

A little later in his prayer, Jesus introduces his disciples into his dialogue with the Father. And here, the language of holiness is explicitly employed:

> Make them holy in truth; your word is truth. As you sent
> me into the world, so have I sent them into the world.
>   (Jn 17:17-18)

In the very same way that Jesus himself was sent by the Father into the world as the bearer of divine holiness, this holiness being both the motive and the goal of his sending, he wants his disciples, after his death, to continue his work. So as he sends them into the world, he asks the Father to equip them with the gift of holiness. And the following verse closes the circle, because we learn that it is through Christ's gift of his life, the final and definitive expression of holiness, that the disciples will receive this holiness in their turn. The passion and death of God's Son are not only the perfect manifestation of God's holiness, but in addition the transmission of this holiness to human beings. Once again we see that holiness, by its very nature, is communicative. Far from being a movement of separation, it sparks a kind of chain reaction:

> And for them I am making myself holy, so that they too
> may be holy in truth.   (Jn 17:19)

And exactly as in chapter 12, the great sign that enables us to conclude that this communication has indeed taken place is the *unity* among the disciples that it makes possible, a consequence of the holiness (here, the "glory") received from the Father by the Son and then communicated to his disciples, so that their life in turn may be a sign for the world:

> ...that all may be one, just as you, Father, are in me and
> I am in you; may they be one in us, so that the world
> may believe that you sent me. I have given them the
> glory which you gave me, that they may be one as we
> are one, I in them and you in me, that they may be per-
> fectly one, so that the world may know that you sent me
> and that you have loved them just as you have loved me.
>   (Jn 17:21-23)

At the end of this extremely profound and intense journey, holiness is revealed unambiguously as the divine energy of a communion.

There is another New Testament book that explores the link between the death of Christ and holiness revealed and communicated. That book is the Letter to the Hebrews, a kind of treatise written for Jewish Christians. The unknown author uses the example of the worship of ancient Israel to explain to his hearers the mission of Christ. For him, the liturgy in the Temple was a kind of "copy" (Heb 8:5; 9:23), a "figure" or "symbol" (9:9), or even a "shadow" or "sketch" (8:5; 10:1) of what Jesus accomplished in reality by his coming. It is not surprising, then, that this writing takes up the vocabulary of sacrifice and applies it to Christ. We should recall that, in the Hebrew Scriptures, a sacrifice is a gift given through the intermediary of a priest to express and reinforce a relationship with God. The one who makes such an offering, as well as the reality which is offered, must be in a state of holiness, for nothing impure can approach God. At the same time, a sacrifice leads to an increase in holiness by creating a deeper communion between believers and their God.

How does such a practice relate to the life of Christ? In a unique way, to such an extent that the old categories break apart and then come together again in an entirely original manner. Instead of multiplicity there is unity, and Christ is both priest and victim of this one sacrifice:

> He does not need to offer sacrifices daily like the high priests, first for his own sins and then for those of the people, for he did this once and for all when he offered himself. (Heb 7:27)

By living for God, Jesus lived a life for others, and this gift of his life, which was ratified by his death on Calvary, is the reality expressed more or less awkwardly by all the offerings that formed part of the worship of ancient Israel. The free self-giving of God's only Son, and not the blood of an animal, acquires a definitive forgiveness for us. Penetrated by God's holiness, we enter into the fullness of a communion with God:

> ...we have been made holy by the offering of the body
> of Jesus Christ once and for all. (...) By a single offer-
> ing he brought to perfection for all time those he is
> making holy.   (Heb 10:10,14; cf. 9:14; 13:12)

This language, not readily comprehensible to us today, uses different categories to express the exact same truth as John's Gospel: the total gift of his life made by Jesus on the cross communicates God's holiness to us in a definitive manner.

Questions for Reflection

1. In our examination of biblical holiness, we found among others the following elements: holiness as a reality which attracts and upsets, able to transform life; a movement towards rather than a separation; a force for healing, forgiveness and reconciliation. How are these elements, as well as other aspects of holiness, present in the supreme act by which Jesus brings to a conclusion his life on earth?

2. How does the Christian reading of Psalm 40 made by the author of the Letter to the Hebrews (Heb 10:1-10) help us to understand the new vision of holiness offered by Jesus Christ?

Communion Rediscovered

12 The entire New Testament, despite the diversity of the theologies found in its pages, leads to the same realization: it is by the total gift of his life, made concrete by his death on the cross, that Jesus expresses fully his identity. He is the Son, whose entire existence consists in a communion of love with his heavenly Father, in a permanent and dynamic attitude of welcoming and giving. He is the Holy One from God, whose life is penetrated by the fire of holiness and who communicates this fire to human beings. It is on the cross, in an experience of absolute dereliction, that this identity shines out most unambiguously.

It is nonetheless true that, seen from the outside, the death of Jesus does not necessarily bear this meaning. Does it not resemble more closely a failure, the victory of violence and hatred, rather than a manifestation of the holiness of a God of love? And we must not forget that, in the face of his imminent death, Christ prayed to the Father to make his act bear fruit. Humanly speaking, once he had given everything by going to the

point of death, Jesus would no longer be capable of accomplishing anything himself.

In other words, death in itself inevitably retains a dark
and scandalous aspect. Jesus thus looks to his Father for an
act that will turn the situation around and reveal the authentic meaning of his death.

Once before in the Gospel, the Father had caused the
glory belonging by right to his Son to be manifested, for a brief
moment and in the presence of three disciples only (Mt 17:1-
9). The event had taken place on "a high mountain" (v. 1), at
a time when Jesus was getting ready to go up to Jerusalem and
expose himself to the violence of his enemies. Confronted with
this "transfiguration" of their Master, the disciples were
"deeply frightened" (v. 6), like Moses before the burning bush
or Isaiah in the Temple. It is not by chance, then, that an identical reaction took place on the third day after the death of
Jesus, when some women visiting his tomb found, not a corpse,
but a messenger from heaven who proclaimed, "He is risen!"
(Mk 16:1-8).

The death of Jesus was thus not the final act of his drama;
it led to a revelation of the mystery of God without parallel in
the history of humankind. The confrontation of the women
and, later, of the group of disciples with the mysterious reality of the resurrection causes perplexity (Lk 24:4), alarm (Mk
16:5), fright (Mk 16:8; Lk 24:5,37), trembling (Mk 16:8; Mt
28:4), bewilderment (Mk 16:8), fear mixed with happiness (Mt
28:8), astonishment (Lk 24:12,41) and finally great joy (Jn
20:20; Lk 24:52). These reactions are understandable because,
in his resurrection, the humanity of Christ is "glorious," in
other words entirely penetrated and transformed by the divine holiness.

By raising his Son from the dead, God lends his hand to

the work of Christ; he establishes the true meaning of this death as the revelation of holiness. At the same time, as a result of his resurrection "by the Spirit of holiness" (Rm 1:4) Jesus is henceforth able to communicate this holiness to his followers without limit. Saint John shows us this communication already on Easter day, in the meeting between the risen Christ and Mary of Magdala (Jn 20:11-18).

Mary had been one of those closest to Jesus during his earthly ministry. Now that he is gone, she naturally imagines that their relationship is over. Overcome by grief and despair, she attempts to rescue from oblivion at least a few fragments of the vanished relationship, some memories. Her life is now turned toward the past, symbolized by the tomb and the corpse, two signs of what once was and is no longer.

This attitude of Mary, as ultimately futile as it is worthy of comprehension and sympathy, keeps her from being fully present to the reality that surrounds her. When she enters the tomb, she does not even notice the presence of heavenly messengers, harbingers of a new day, and in her obsessive search for a dead body she mistakes Jesus himself for the gardener. Only when Christ calls her by name is the spell broken: the relationship is restored, and all at once she lands back in the present. And twice, the text uses the expression "she turns round" (vv. 14, 16), a verb used in Hebrew to refer to conversion of heart. Confronted with the presence of the Risen Lord who calls her, Mary responds with a movement from the very depths of her being, leaving behind her past life to enter into a new beginning with Christ.

For all that, she still has another step to take. The restored relationship cannot be a carbon-copy of the previous one. Jesus is now risen, in other words completely transfigured by God's holiness, and so a communion with him is more than ever open, inclusive. If she wants to remain in that communion, Mary Magdalene must surrender all claims to possession and set out towards others in the footsteps of the Living One:

> Jesus said to her, "Let go of me.... Go instead to my brothers and tell them: I am going up to my Father and your Father, to my God and your God." (Jn 20:17)

The relationship with the risen Christ turns the disciple into an apostle or an evangelist, a living word that calls others, in God's name, to leave behind all forms of arrogant or despairing self-reliance and to enter into that same communion. This is shown once again later that same day. When he joins the apostles on the evening of Easter Day, the risen Christ speaks these words to them: "'Peace to you! As the Father has sent me, so I am sending you.' When he said these words he breathed on them and said, 'Receive the Holy Spirit: if you forgive anyone's sins, they are forgiven...'" (Jn 20:21-23; cf. 17:18). Holiness in person, like a gentle breeze, will propel them along the roads of the world as witnesses to a forgiveness always offered.

This communication of holiness as the consequence of a relationship with the Risen Christ finds its normative expression fifty days later, during the feast of Pentecost. The Holy Spirit is sent upon the disciples gathered together in the upper room in Jerusalem (Ac 2). It is significant that this transformation of the disciples is indicated by "tongues as of fire [which] came down upon each one of them" (Ac 2:3). In this way, the words of the Baptizer are fulfilled concerning a baptism "in the Holy Spirit and fire" (Lk 3:16; Ac 1:5). The earth is finally set ablaze with the fire of God's holiness (Lk 12:49-50). But as the prophet Jeremiah had realized centuries earlier (Jr 20:9), this fire burns in the human heart, transforming people from the inside out and enabling them to speak to others in God's name.

Question for Reflection

1. In the following texts, Saint Paul speaks of the death and resurrection of Jesus not as a simple past event but as a reality that transforms the existence of believers here and now: Romans 6:3-11 and 8:11; 2 Corinthians 4:6-18; Philippians 3:3-14. How do these texts help us to understand the importance of the Easter mystery for our life today?

Becoming
a Person

13 In trying to understand the notion of holiness in the Bible, we took as our starting-point an *experience* that a human being can have. This experience was essentially an encounter with the Mystery at the heart of life, an event that leads people off their beaten paths and ushers them into a new and unsettling world. Then, in our investigation of the life of the people of Israel, the *meaning* of this experience gradually became clearer; holiness acquired more precise contours. Finally, the New Testament tells us that in the coming of Jesus Christ, God revealed and communicated to the fullest extent possible the secret of his being. In following this road, we discover the progression of God's ongoing self-communication as it is found in the Bible. Holiness leaves heaven and comes down to earth, entering ever more deeply into the warp and woof of the human condition. Its center of gravity shifts from specific experiences to a relationship lived out over time. Similarly, perceived at first from the outside, holiness is seen in the end to be a reality of the inner life.

Now, at the end of this double movement of descent and interiorization, we are finally in a position to reflect on the holy as it affects our own lives. Let us look first at the beginning of the letter to the Ephesians, the address of the letter, which identifies the sender and the recipients:

> Paul, apostle of Christ Jesus by the will of God, to the saints and faithful in Christ Jesus.
> (Eph 1:1; cf. Ph 1:1; 2 Cor 1:1)

Paul writes to the *saints,* the holy men and women in Ephesus.[1] And who are these holy people? The rest of the phrase tell us: the faithful, those who believe in Christ Jesus. In other words, the apostle uses the expression "the saints" not to refer to a group of "super-Christians" more committed or closer to God than the others, but simply to identify the members of the Christian community to whom he is writing. He says "the saints" where today we would say "the Christians."

In the New Testament, therefore, the saints are not a part of God's people but a way of speaking of that people as such (cf. Ex 19:6). And we never find the expression used in the singular to refer to one man or woman: a person is holy because he or she belongs to God's holy people. Far from being a characteristic of an individual which distinguishes him or her from others, holiness involves personal relationships which link human beings to God and make of them a community.

The beginning of the first letter to the Corinthians gives a more precise meaning to this term as it is applied to Christians:

---

[1] It is unfortunate that, in English, the personal noun corresponding to the (Germanic) adjective "holy" is "saint," which came into the language from Latin via French. This makes it harder for English-speakers, alone among the major European languages, to grasp spontaneously the unity between the two. A saint *is* a holy man or woman; the difference is purely verbal.

Paul, called to be an apostle of Christ Jesus by the will
of God, and Sosthenes the brother, to the Church of
God which is in Corinth, to those made holy in Christ
Jesus and called to be holy....   (1 Cor 1:1-2)

"Made holy in Christ Jesus and called to be holy." This
phrase sums up admirably the two principal axes of holiness
in the life of believers.

First and foremost, holiness is a *gift*. The Bible repeats
over and over that God alone is holy. As a result, it is formally
impossible for human beings to become holy by their own
endeavors. God alone can make them holy. And we have seen
that this is precisely what God wishes to do: the God of the
Bible intends to communicate his holiness to human beings.
This communication takes place across the centuries, in the
ongoing history told in the Bible which culminates in the life,
death and resurrection of God's only Son. In Jesus Christ,
God's holiness becomes fully accessible to us.

The accounts of the resurrection appearances of Jesus
show us how holiness is transmitted. No physical, mechanical
or economic images can adequately do justice to this process;
it involves of necessity a *personal* encounter. Each and every
Christian occupies the place which was that of Mary of
Magdala beside the tomb of Jesus (cf. Jn 20:11-18). This encounter is recapitulated in Christian *baptism*. It is true that, for
those of us who were baptized as infants, the fullest and deepest meaning of the sacrament remains veiled. To understand
it, we must keep in mind the way in which baptism was practiced in New Testament times: it was a step taken above all by
adults.

Like Mary, the future believer is searching. She may be
actively searching for a deeper significance in her life, a Reality that is more real; or perhaps a desire from elsewhere has

been awakened within her without her knowing how or why. This search and this desire will assume a specific form according to her particular history and mentality. At given moments, they may correspond to names like "curiosity," "nostalgia" or even "desolation" and lead to a great variety of decisions, experiences and encounters. Then, one day, a word touches the very depths of her being: Christ has called her by name. The voice she hears at that moment is clearly distinguishable from all other voices. It is the Word by which she was created, the only one able to enter the most secret sanctuary of her self, to awaken a response from her innermost soul. In the Gospel according to Saint John, Jesus expresses this by the simple image of a shepherd:

> The one who comes in through the gate is the shepherd of the sheep. The gatekeeper opens the gate for him, and the sheep listen to his voice. He calls his own sheep by name and leads them out. When he has brought all his own out, he walks in front of them, and the sheep follow him because they recognize his voice. They will not follow a stranger, but rather will run away from him, because they do not recognize the voice of strangers.... I am the good shepherd; I know my sheep and my sheep know me.... My sheep listen to my voice; I know them and they follow me, and I give them eternal life.
>
> (Jn 10:2-5,14,27-28)

The call of the one true shepherd causes a radical turnabout in the life of a human being, a *metanoia* by which he leaves his old life behind to enter into a new life with Christ. This change is so radical that Saint Paul does not hesitate to compare it to dying:

> Are you unaware that those of us who were baptized into Christ Jesus were baptized into his death? We have there-

fore been buried with him through baptism into his
death...   (Rm 6:3-4a)

When we looked at the experience of holiness in the
Hebrew Scriptures, our "Old Testament," we saw that an ineluctable aspect of it was, for the person involved, the *fear* of
being pulled out of his habitual world. Carried to its extreme,
this leads to the affirmation that "no one can see [God] and
live" (Ex 33:20), since holiness is beyond all human capacities. And yet, human beings desire above all else this encounter with the Holy One (Ex 33:18; cf. Ps 42:2; Jn 14:8). They
thus seem to have been created for a fulfillment which is not
only beyond their reach, but which would annihilate them.
In the New Testament, we find the solution to this enigma.
The gift of holiness which Jesus Christ gives human beings
does in fact lead to a death, but, just as for Christ himself, this
death is not God's last word:

> ...so that just as Christ was raised from the dead by the
> Father's glory, we too might live a new life. (Rm 6:4b)

Through Jesus, we know that holiness (here "glory") is
above all something life-giving. It was the power of the divine
holiness in him that made his death on the cross not an end
but a road to Life (Rm 1:4). In the same way, the gift of holiness in us makes possible a new life that is "eternal," that is, a
participation in God's own life.

What are the characteristics of this new life? Let us listen to Saint Paul once again:

> For the love of Christ urges us onward, with the thought
> that one died for all and so all have died And he died
> for all so that the living should no longer live for them-
> selves, but for the one who died and rose for them.
> (2 Cor 5:14-15)

Here, the life a believer leaves behind is referred to as "living for oneself" and the new life that begins "living for Christ." It is essentially a question of *belonging*, of the foundations upon which someone's identity is built:

> None of us live for ourselves, and none of us die for ourselves. For if we live, we live for the Lord, and if we die, we die for the Lord. So whether we live or die, we are the Lord's.   (Rm 14:7-8)

When Saint Paul describes baptism as a dying with Christ, it should now be obvious that he is not speaking of physical death, but rather the disappearance of the "old self" (Rm 6:6; Col 3:9; Eph 4:22) which was looking for an illusory autonomy (cf. Jn 12:25; Lk 9:23-25; 17:33) and which, setting itself up as the center of its own small universe, was doomed to accomplish works of division and destruction (Col 3:5-9; Eph 4:17-31; Gal 5:19-21). Having died through faith and baptism to a life with one's own self as beginning and end, believers are renewed in the image of Christ; henceforth they live through and for God and others (Rm 6:9-11). Having died as solitary beings, they are alive through and for communion.

It is important to realize that this change is not a simple ethical amelioration, an increase in generosity; it involves rather a total re-creation of human existence. To describe it, we can use two everyday words to which we attribute a more precise meaning.[2] Let us call Saint Paul's "old self," in other

---

[2] Such a method (which Buber, *I and Thou*, pp. 111-115, also follows, though the word "ego" and not "individual" is used as in the English translation; see note 7, p. 111) makes comprehension easier, but is not without its drawbacks. From now on, in these pages, we must remember that the terms are used in a technical and not an everyday sense. On the other hand, it is significant that the word "person" was strongly influenced by the theological reflections of the first Christian centuries. See the article of the Ortho-

words someone who looks for their identity in themselves alone, an *individual.* An individual wants to be, whether naively or perversely, his own source; he views his own self as the center of the universe.

On the other hand there is what we can call a *person.* A person is someone who finds his or her identity in a relationship, someone who is *responsible.* A person lives through a ceaseless exchange with others, an exchange made up of welcoming and giving. And when we have a personal relationship with God, the absolute Source, then obviously welcoming takes precedence on the human side. We are contingent beings; in order to give, we must first of all receive. These terms allow us to sum up our discoveries in this way: in a relationship with the Risen Lord expressed through faith and baptism, a human being dies as an individual in order to be reborn as a person.

At this point, we cannot fail to notice the connection between the new life of baptized Christians and the identity of Christ himself. As the Son, Christ is the person *par excellence.* By his attempt to discover God's will which is his nourishment (Jn 4:34) and by his response of filial love or "obedience" (Jn 14:31), his entire existence is defined by a communion with the one he calls Abba. Christ, therefore, transforms us into beings similar to himself — beings who recognize God as their loving Abba (Rm 8:15; Gal 4:6), so that he becomes "the firstborn of many brothers and sisters" (Rm 8:29).

Believers experience in their own life the two dimensions of personal existence, the "negative" and the "positive" ones, which we identified in the words of Christ (see p. 78):

---

dox Metropolitan, John Zizioulas, "Personhood and Being," in his work, *Being as Communion* (Crestwood, NY: St. Vladimir's Seminary Press, 1985), pp. 27-65. See also Philippe Cormier, *Généalogie de Personne* (Paris: Critérion, 1995), especially pp. 161-238: "[As a person,] a human being can only be considered from the viewpoint of God" (p. 209).

Everything is yours, whether Paul or Apollo or Cephas
or the world or life or death or the present or the future. Everything is yours, but you are Christ's and Christ
is God's.   (1 Cor 3:21-23)

Insofar as their existence is rooted in this sharing of life
with God through Christ, believers possess everything: in biblical language, they are *heirs* to all the riches of God (Gal 3:15—
4:7; Rm 8:17; Heb 6:12,17; 9:15). Outside of this communion,
however, they are nothing and have nothing. Here we find the
authentic basis of Christian humility — the conviction that
everything is a gift.

The gift of an existence-in-relationship is in fact the gift
of God's holiness in person, the Holy Spirit. We have seen that
the account of the first Christian Pentecost dramatizes explicitly this communication of holiness. "There appeared to them
tongues as of fire, which divided and came down upon each
one of them. And they were all filled with the Holy Spirit..."
(Ac 2:3-4). The risen Christ sends upon the disciples Holiness
personified, God's Spirit, who engraves on their hearts, in letters of fire, the Law of the new covenant. But far from being a
single, detached event, what happens on Pentecost in Jerusalem is the beginning of a process which runs through the
entire history of the Christian Church. The fire which Christ
kindles at that moment (cf. Lk 12:49) is passed on from one
person to another across the centuries. It reaches each believer
above all through baptism (cf. Ac 2:38). That is perhaps why
Saint John can call this sacrament "an anointing from the Holy
One" (1 Jn 2:20).[3]

---

[3] In fact, this expression remains somewhat enigmatic. Does it refer to water
baptism, to an anointing with oil preceding or accompanying water baptism, or is it a simple image to describe the action of the Spirit?

To describe the gift of holiness which believers receive, Saint Paul borrows an expression from the worship of his people. For the Jews of the biblical period, the Temple in Jerusalem was the principal dwelling-place of God's holiness. They were aware, of course, that the God of Israel did not live in a house built by human hands (2 S 7:5ff.; 1 K 8:27; Is 66:1; cf. 57:15). And yet the Temple, constructed in the form of concentric circles around its center, the "Holy of Holies," played a predominant role in the piety of the Jewish people. They journeyed there to enter into the presence of the Holy One, to offer sacrifices, to celebrate festivals. A song like Psalm 122 expresses well the happiness of the faithful on pilgrimage towards the Temple:

> I rejoiced with those who said to me,
> "Let us go to the house of the Lord." (...)
> For the sake of the house of the Lord our God,
> I will seek your prosperity.
>
> (Ps 122:1,9)

Jesus' relationship to the Temple is more complex. On the one hand, he has nothing against the building as such. He even honors it, teaching there (Mk 11:27; 12:35; Jn 7:14; 8:2; etc.), healing the sick (Mt 21:14), and on one occasion cleansing it by a dramatic gesture along the lines of the prophets of the past (Mt 21:12; Jn 2:14-16; cf. Ml 3:1-4; Zc 14:21; Jr 7:1-15), a way of pointing out the true vocation of the sanctuary which is to be "a house of prayer for all the nations" (Mk 11:17; Is 56:7). On the other hand, the very presence of Jesus relativizes the Temple's claim to be the privileged place to encounter the Holy One. From now on, this institution is no longer numbered among the ultimate realities (Lk 21:5-6; cf. Mt 12:6; Mk 15:38). It is not surprising, then, that those who

imagine that their security and their authority are indissolu-
bly linked to the Temple feel threatened by the prophet from
Nazareth. For them it is an easy task to deform some enigmatic
words he spoke regarding the Temple and to turn them into
one of the main charges against him during his trial:

> We heard him say, "I will destroy this sanctuary made
> by human hands and in three days I will build another
> one, not made by human hands." (Mk 14:58; cf. Ac 24:6)

John's Gospel explains the true import of these words:
"But he was talking about the sanctuary of his body" (Jn 2:21),
the earthly dwelling of divine holiness.

Saint Paul takes up this last line of thought in his first
letter to the Corinthians:

> Do you not know that you are God's temple, and the
> Spirit of God dwells in you? If someone destroys God's
> temple, God will destroy that person. For God's temple
> is holy, and that temple is you.
>   (1 Cor 3:16-17; cf. 2 Cor 6:16; Eph 2:21-22)

You are the place where holiness resides, he says to the
Christians, for God's Spirit dwells within you as the source of
your new life. Here Paul's perspective is communal and not
individual, for those who are destroying the Temple are
people who foment divisions in the community of believers
(cf. 1 Cor 1:11-13; 3:3). To make them see the momentous
consequences of their behavior, Paul compares it to an act of
sacrilege, which in the ancient world was a particularly seri-
ous crime, punishable by death.

A little later in the same letter, Paul takes up this image
again but this time uses it in a personal way:

> Do you not know that your body is a temple of the Holy
> Spirit in you, which you have from God, and you do not
> belong to yourselves?   (1 Cor 6:19)

In their concrete existence in the world (that is often the meaning of "the body" in Paul's writings), believers carry around God's Holy Spirit like a treasure in a jar of clay (2 Cor 4:7). They must remember, then, that they no longer belong to themselves but that their lives have a significance that goes far beyond what is under their own purview and control. The expression "a temple of the Holy Spirit" is thus linked to the change from the "old self" to the "new humanity" in Christ. Bearers of the gift of holiness, we no longer live in a self-contained, autonomous world. Our entire existence becomes personal, in other words a movement of welcoming and giving which has its starting-point within. Believers thus experience as well a radical reversal of perspectives in that their bodies do not enclose a "private" space. By becoming the dwelling-place of the Holy Spirit (cf. 2 Tm 1:14), their hearts are no longer their private possession, but rather an opening from within, a kind of "window on eternity."

Question for Reflection

1. How do the following texts help us to discover what it means to be a responsible person in the image of Christ: Philippians 2:1-11; Luke 12:35-48; Romans 12; Hebrews 10:1-10?

The Call
To Holiness

14 "Called to be holy" (1 Cor 1:2). If holiness in human beings is above all a gift, this gift is, just as it was for Mary, at the same time a call. Christ calls us to find our identity in a relationship with him, to become *persons,* beings-in-relation. He invites us to be *responsible,* to make our lives a response to the gift/call we have received. As Jesus explains in the parable of the talents (Mt 25:14ff.), God's gifts are not like human ones: the only way to keep them is to put them into practice immediately. The gift of holiness which comes to us from the Father through the passover of his Son and which consists of the inner presence of the Holy Spirit is like a seed meant to grow and bear fruit. Or to shift the image, the tiny flame of holiness placed in our hearts must use everything that comes its way for fuel in order to grow into a conflagration that consumes all of our self-centeredness and radiates warmth and light around us. And this, to be sure, is the work of an entire lifetime. The gift received in the one-time event of baptism is the starting-point of an endless process, by which we go "from one beginning to another in beginnings without end" (St. Gregory of Nyssa, fourth century).[1]

In other words, if we *are* saints because of the presence of the Holy Spirit within us, it is up to us to *become* saints by translating this presence into the choices and acts of our day-to-day life. The most important question, then, is this: How can we express concretely in our existence this new life rooted in a relationship with the Trinitarian God? The New Testament gives a single response to this question, but expresses it in many different ways. Perhaps the first letter of Saint John puts it most clearly:

> Beloved, if God has so loved us, we too should love one another. No one has ever seen God. If we love one another, God remains in us and his love has come to perfection in us.... If someone says, "I love God," and hates his brother or sister, that person is a liar, because whoever does not love the brother or sister whom they see cannot love the God whom they do not see.
>
> (1 Jn 4:11-12,20)

For the Gospel, the authenticity of our relations with God can only be verified by the relations we have with the human beings around us. Belonging to God means at the same time discovering that we are truly members of the human community, that the connections between us are real and not just ideological, something in our heads. Responding to God

---

[1] This spiritual process is the foundation of the logic of the Church's *sacraments*, a logic which is absolutely unique. A sacrament is not simply a starting-point, still less a mere symbolic expression of a reality of faith. On a deeper level, it is an encounter with Christ in his passover who gives *everything*... but in embryo. And this "everything" requires all of life in order to reach full maturity. Thus no human concept or model can adequately define what a sacrament is.

means being responsible for all those whom God has entrusted to us. "Insofar as you have done it for one of the least of these my brothers and sisters, you have done it for me" (Mt 25:40).

In his writings, Saint John defines the form of human behavior which best reflects God's holiness as *love*, a love which in his eyes is essentially reciprocal ("one another, brothers and sisters"). We reach the same destination by a different route if we consider the Gospel's interpretation of the commandment which sums up the "Law of Holiness" in the Torah of Moses:

> Be holy because I, the Lord your God, am holy.
> (Lv 19:2)

In two of the Synoptic Gospels, Jesus gives an implicit commentary on this verse. In Luke we read:

> Be merciful, just as your Father is merciful.
> (Lk 6:36)

And in Matthew:

> You will be perfect as your heavenly Father is perfect.
> (Mt 5:48)

If we examine this last verse in its context (Mt 5:43-48), it is clear that the "perfection" in question does not consist in a complete absence of faults, an irreproachable moral rigor, but above all in a love which goes to the point of embracing even those who do not love us in return. In a word, it refers to that perfection of love which is called forgiveness.

In these verses, then, Jesus interprets holiness in terms of mercy, of a love which is not invalidated or destroyed by the refusal of the other person to accept it. Although God's love looks for reciprocity in order to be "brought to completion" (1 Jn 4:12; 2:5), it is nevertheless not determined by the attitude or the behavior of the recipient; it is pure generosity. And Saint Paul reconciles the two lines by showing in his turn the close connection between holiness and love:

> May the Lord make you increase and abound in love for one another and for all, just as we do for you. In so doing may he keep your hearts blameless in holiness before our God and Father for the coming of our Lord Jesus with all his saints.   (1 Th 3:12-13)

The life of believers is rooted in holiness to the extent that love grows greater among the members of the community as well as for those who do not yet belong to it.

If a holy life is above all a life of love and forgiveness, that explains why, from the beginning, Christians did not live their faith exclusively in a relationship with Christ but formed bonds among themselves as well. Already during Jesus' life on earth, his disciples constituted a community which had a certain structure. After the resurrection, this community life developed and spread. Why do we live out our faith with others? First of all, it is true that the demanding life which Jesus asks of his followers is easier to live if we are not alone but have the support of others. The Gospel asks us to go contrary to so many habits and prejudices of the surrounding world that left to ourselves we are in danger of losing courage and hope.

The true justification of Christian community, however, is much more profound. A shared existence is the very expression of the new life of the Holy Spirit communicated to us by Christ. Our personal relationship with God through Christ is lived out in our personal relationships with others, by the fact of belonging to a community, the community of believers.

Thus the fact that, from the very start, Christians came

together in a community at one and the same time local and universal, called the Church (from the Greek word *ekklēsia,* "gathering, congregation"), is in no way a coincidence or an optional element of their faith. It is the inescapable consequence of it. Being a person means discovering one's identity through belonging to a communion that is rooted in God's call and that tends by its own dynamism to expand until its dimensions coincide with the entire human family, not to say the whole of God's creation. And the Church, the community of those who have already responded to the call through faith and baptism, is the "sacramental" concretization of this universal communion in the process of becoming.

The New Testament expresses the reality of the Church by a constellation of images. The first letter of Saint Peter returns to the image of the Temple, an excellent way of bringing together all the different dimensions of holiness in the life of believers — holiness as gift and holiness as call, personal and communal holiness:

> As you come close to him, the living stone, rejected by human beings but chosen and precious in God's eyes, you too, as living stones, are being built up as a spiritual dwelling for a holy priesthood, offering spiritual sacrifices pleasing to God through Jesus Christ.
>
> (1 P 2:4-5)

In this new Temple, each of us is a "living stone," and with Christ as cornerstone we form a spiritual edifice. In other words, God's holiness does not reside in a material building but in the community of believers (cf. 1 Cor 3:16-17). Then the author changes the image. In addition to being stones in this new Temple, we are the priests who offer sacrifices inside the house! Here then, the call to put holiness into practice is expressed by the image of offering sacrifices. These sacrifices are not, of course, goats and sheep but "spiritual sacrifices"; in the steps of Christ himself, under the impulsion of the Holy Spirit, our entire life is called to be a gift to God.

How do we make of our lives a "sacrifice"? A key text of Saint Paul's sets us on the right road:

> I encourage you then, my sisters and brothers, because of God's mercy, to make your bodies living sacrifices, holy and pleasing to God — that is your spiritual worship. Do not conform to this world, but be transformed by renewing your way of thinking, so that you may discern what God wants, what is good and pleasing and perfect.   (Rm 12:1-2)

Instead of giving us a list of do's and don'ts, a series of rules to put into practice blindly, Paul urges us not to follow the fashions and values of present-day society but to seek to discern God's will for ourselves. This is essentially a call to act responsibly rather than to follow the crowd. In thus relying on believers' own powers of discernment, Paul roots his confidence in the gift of the Spirit which they have received:

> God has revealed it to us by the Spirit, for the Spirit sounds everything, even the depths of God. For what human being knows what is in a person better than the inner spirit of that person? In the same way, no one knows God's affairs better than the Spirit of God. For our part we have not received the spirit of the world but the Spirit which comes from God, that we might know the free gifts God has given us. And we speak about them not with words of learned human teaching but as the Spirit teaches, interpreting spiritual things to the spiritual. Human beings who remain on a natural level cannot deal with what comes from God's Spirit; it makes no

sense to them. They cannot understand it because it must be judged spiritually. But spiritual people judge everything and nobody judges them. For "who knows the way the Lord thinks, who can instruct him?" But we, for our part, have Christ's way of thinking. (1 Cor 2:10-16)

Pay attention to this presence of God in the depths of your hearts, says Paul in effect; it will show you the road to follow. And Saint John reminds us that this inner presence is nothing other than the Spirit of holiness. In discussing baptism, he writes to his community, "...you have an anointing from the Holy One, and all of you know" (1 Jn 2:20; cf. 2:27; 1 Th 4:9). It must immediately be added that the outlook of the apostles is resolutely communal. They are not at all preaching an ethical individualism. It is all together, as members of a community where each person has received a particular gift, that Christians will discover what God wants. Those who use their own inspirations as a pretext for distancing themselves from their brothers and sisters only prove by their behavior that the spirit they possess does not come from God (1 Jn 2:19; cf. 2:11). Discernment in community cannot be dispensed with (1 Jn 4:1).

For the letter to the Hebrews, the "sacrifice" of Christians has two aspects: *prayer* and *the sharing of goods* (Heb 13,15-16). Practicing holiness thus means living as far as possible both aspects of communion — communion with God and communion among humans. And finally, the letter to the Ephesians defines sacrifice, the gift of self, as a life of love in imitation of God as manifested in the example of Christ:

> Become imitators of God, as his dear children, and walk along the road of love, just as Christ loved you and gave himself for us, a sweet-smelling offering and sacrifice to God. (Eph 5:1-2)

To sum up, if holiness is above all a gift from God, the gift of God's Holy Spirit, in the life of believers it is likewise a call to live in such a way that the gift expands until it permeates their entire life. And for the New Testament, this is not only a personal challenge. The call to holiness is addressed to the Christian community as a whole. The Church is called to be, like ancient Israel and in an even more inward fashion, a "holy people" that by its life offers the world the image of a God who is communion, a "temple" that brings together all human beings to serve and worship the Lord, a "burning bush" that places itself on the roadside where all people pass to awaken them to the adventure of holiness.

Questions for Reflection

1. In 2 Corinthians 3:4—4:6, Saint Paul explains how God's glory shines in the world through his apostolic ministry, even more fully than in the life of Moses. Then, in 4:7-15, he describes concretely what this means for him. What light does this text shed on our own spiritual journey in the steps of Christ? How do our lives let God's holiness shine through?
2. How does the text from the Desert Father given on page xv of this book help us to understand the call to holiness?
3. What can we do so that our Christian communities can be "burning bushes" that allow others to encounter God's holiness?

In the Family
of God

15 The New Testament tells us unambiguously that those
who respond to Christ's call and find their identity in a
communion with God live out this life-in-communion
through their relationships with the human beings
around them, and in a special way with those who are
responding to the same call. Together they form a
community known as the Church, a community called to
be, by the shared life of its members, an incontrovertible
sign of the new life rooted in the communion of the God
who is Father, Son and Spirit. "This is how all will know
that you are my disciples: by the love you have for one
another" (Jn 13:35; cf. 17:21,23).

This community is in no way an exclusive club or a
privileged elite: God offers his love to all (cf 1 Tm 2:4),
but those who have already heard the call are led by it to
translate their new personal identity into the way they
live with others. And where there is reciprocity, true
community life can spring up. We must immediately
add, of course, that the Christian Church, existing as it
does at the heart of a history characterized by refusals

and divisions, never corresponds exactly to what it truly is. Saint Matthew's Gospel expresses this most clearly, in the parables of the weeds and the wheat mingled in a field (Mt 13:24-30) and the net "that brings in all kinds of things" (Mt 13:47-50). Precisely because it is founded on the discovery of true freedom, which follows from a relationship of love with a personal God, and then among human persons, the Church cannot manifest itself as a monolithic bloc without betraying its identity. Nonetheless, it is within the community of those who are faithful to Christ that the leaven of holiness is at work, discreetly but efficiently raising the dough of the human condition. Amazing as such a statement may seem, this community is the only place in the world where a life that is both fully personal and fully universal can come to full flower.

One of the images by which the New Testament describes the Church is that of the *family*. Modern societies are pluralistic, possessing a myriad of institutions and groupings that bring people together and provide them with identity and security. In the ancient world, however, family ties were by far the most important. People could be said to exist, so to speak, to the extent that they found their place within an extended family. In this context, it is not surprising that the early Christians described the change wrought in them by baptism as the entry into a new family, the universal family of God.

Thus the first believers in Christ were led almost spontaneously to use the vocabulary of the family to speak about their life. They called themselves "brothers and sisters" (Ac 1:15; 6:3; Rm 16:1; 1 Cor 16:12,20; Col 1:1-2, etc.). Here we may have a recollection of some words of the Risen Christ (Mt 28:10; Jn 20:17). In any case, Christians saw themselves, through their faith in Christ and because of the gift of the Holy Spirit, as having entered into the same relationship which Christ had with God. Henceforth they too could fittingly address God as their "Abba" (Gal 4:6; Rm 8:15) and consider Jesus as their older brother (Rm 8:29; Heb 2:10-18). As a result of their communion with the Son, they became sons and daughters of God.

In his preaching during his life on earth, Jesus used the same language to speak of the radical new departure required of those who would follow his call:

> Whoever loves their father or mother more than me is not worthy of me. And whoever loves their son or daughter more than me is not worthy of me. (Mt 10:37)

It should be obvious that Jesus was not advising his disciples to stop loving or caring about their close relatives. The operative word here is not "love" but "more." It is above all a question of priorities: the disciples now form part of the universal family of God, at the heart of which Jesus is the representative of the heavenly Father. All other relationships, even the closest ones in human terms, must be re-evaluated in the light of this new belonging. Human institutions and ties, though they do not lose their importance, are now relativized in favor of a more important and more urgent reality (cf. also Mt 12:46-50; Lk 9:59-62).

In addition, if in certain cases there is a break in a relationship, this is never an end in itself but is rather the other side of a greater and more encompassing unity. This is clear from Jesus' reply when Peter asks him, "We have left everything and followed you; what then will we have?" (Mt 19:27):

> All who have left houses or brothers or sisters or father or mother or children or fields on account of my name will receive much more and will inherit eternal life.
> (Mt 19:29)

A break with a reality of one's previous life, however painful it may be at the time, has meaning only as "the momentary, insignificant trial that brings about in us an exorbitant, eternal weight of glory" (2 Cor 4:17). Looked at from the other side, it is nothing other than the entry into the universal family of God, where there are hundreds of brothers and sisters (cf. Mk 10:30) and where the vast current of community life never runs dry.

Within this great family, personal life, the life of a being-in-relation, can be lived out in a host of different ways. The New Testament insists over and over again that the unity of a communion has nothing to do with uniformity. Each baptized person has received a new name "that no one knows except the one who receives it" (Rv 2:17). Starting from their own gifts and limits, they are called to make use of their freedom to find their own unique place within the community of believers. What keeps everything together is a common Source:

> There is a variety of spiritual gifts, but the same Spirit.
> There is a variety of ways of serving, but the same Lord.
> There is a variety of ways of working, but the same God working all in all.   (1 Cor 12:4-6)

And also a common goal:

> To each person a manifestation of the Spirit is given for the common good.   (1 Cor 12:7)

Our personal identity can never be a pretext for exalting ourselves at the expense of others, nor is it a possession to be clung to jealously. On the contrary, it is a gift to receive and to put into practice so that it can bear fruit in an ever increasing responsibility towards others:

Each person, according to the gift he or she has received, should serve others, like good stewards of one variegated gift of God. (1 P 4:10)

Questions for Reflection

1. The New Testament describes the Church both as a "holy people" (1 P 2:9) and as a mixed reality (Mt 13:24-30,47-50). Can our communities be witnesses to God's holiness without at the same time becoming a closed circle of the "pure"? How can we bring together comprehensiveness and a focus on the essential? What can we do so that openness does not lead to leveling or dispersion?
2. For the Jews, the Passover celebration is a family holiday (Ex 12:3-4). How did Jesus transform it to make it the celebration of God's new family (Lk 22:7-20; 1 Cor 10:16-17)? What can we do so that our Eucharistic celebrations reflect more clearly our identity as this universal family?
3. How does the image of the human body (Rm 12:4-13; 1 Cor 12:12-30) enable Saint Paul to relate unity and diversity in the life of Christians? What does it mean for us "to be members of one another" (Rm 12:5)? What keeps unity from turning into uniformity, diversity into distance or division?

Celibacy and Marriage

16 Our investigations have led to significant results. Holiness in human life means above all living as a person, a being-in-relation. Rooted in a communion with God, sons and daughters in the Son, believers leave all false autonomy behind. They manifest their new identity by belonging to a community in which each person occupies a unique place by reason of their particular limits and gifts. By its nature, communion destroys neither freedom nor creativity. Equally distant from the exaltation of the individual on the one hand and sterile conformity on the other, it traces out a narrow path where one's personal identity comes to full fruition in the gift of oneself to others.

But if there are as many ways of being a person as there are human beings, it is also true that we can identify major life-choices that take up the yes for life spoken to Christ in baptism, in order to apply it to a particular form of life with others. There are two principal life-choices of this sort. One is a commitment to celibacy for the sake of Christ and the Gospel; the other is Christian marriage.

Christ's call asks every man and woman for a radical response; baptism involves a *metanoia* by which we leave our former way of life behind in order to join the universal family of God. This change does not invalidate what was positive in our old life but inevitably relativizes it. Our priorities shift. To express this shift of priorities, some people find that they are called to a life that requires them in advance to "leave" their spouse in a tangible fashion (Lk 18:29; cf. Mt 19:12), in the sense that they renounce all intention of starting their own human family. In this way, they make a choice that expresses in the most concrete way possible the absolute priority of the universal family of God.

Such a decision may be made, for example, in order to accept a special form of ministry in the Church calling for a particular kind of availability. It is no secret that for centuries, the Catholic Church in the West has linked the episcopal and presbyterial ministry to celibacy. But even where there is no explicit link in this sense, some forms of service call upon those who undertake them to give up other definitive commitments, not so much for outward, practical motives as for inward ones. Already in ancient Israel, the prophet Jeremiah had apparently discovered such a call (Jr 16:1-2), and no doubt the most important example is that of Jesus himself. Others are called to join a family, sometimes referred to as a monastic or religious community, that is not founded upon particular human ties but which tries to symbolize in miniature the universal family of God.

Like every step undertaken because of the Gospel, the choice of celibacy has no value in itself, but only in the context of a global response to a call from Christ. First of all, it can never be justified in purely utilitarian terms: even if in some cases it allows for more flexibility in the exercise of practical service, in the final analysis it is an expression of an exclusive love for Christ, which can only be truly understood by the one to whom it is given (cf. Mt 19:11). In the second place, as in all realities of faith, the need to give something up is for the sake of a greater good, here that of expressing by one's life the priority of the universal family of God. In the third place, the commitment to celibacy, like every Christian commitment, is not "for" the one who makes it. A life of celibacy for Christ has sign-value; it is one specific kind of Gospel radicalism offered to the whole of the Christian community and the human family. In other words, if Christ calls some women and men to live in this way, it is not at all in order to create an elite in the Church, a group of "first-class Christians" who would be distinguished from "ordinary" ones. It is rather because the Church as a whole needs people and places where the absolute call meant for every Christian, and normally lived out in a hidden way in the midst of the problems and confusion of ordinary life, is manifested more visibly, like a city set on the top of a hill (cf. Mt 5:14).

And finally, those who live the commitment to celibacy for the sake of Christ and the Gospel do so, like every believer, out of their own human poverty. They know that, in order to give, they need to receive the necessary strength from God. Far from being heroes exempt from difficulties and struggles, they constantly have to draw from prayer and sharing with others the energy of holiness that will enable them to remain faithful in a world where their witness can easily be viewed by others as an aberration or a form of self-indulgence.

And yet, even if the choice of celibacy is not understood in depth by the majority, it has the advantage of asking a question by its very nature. Such a lifestyle has sign-value precisely because is not normal outside of faith in Christ; it makes people think. The incomprehension to which it gives rise is a call to deepen one's understanding. The same thing is not true for the other life-choice that takes up the yes of baptism, Christian marriage. Marriage is a human institution found in all societies; there is apparently nothing specifically Christian about it.[1] In addition, the forms of marriage as a sociological reality vary greatly according to time and place; in the relatively few Bible texts that deal with this topic, it is sometimes difficult to distinguish what is essential and what is conditioned by the historical context.

For these reasons and others, the Christian meaning of the commitment to marriage has often been neglected. Married couples have usually been considered "lay people," which meant for the popular mind "ordinary" or even "second-class" believers. This was a most unfortunate evolution, due to various factors outside the scope of this book. Suffice it to say that whoever listens closely to what the Bible has to say about this topic discovers that, when it is lived out to the full, the commitment of marriage expresses admirably the essential aspects of the new life of communion offered by Jesus Christ.

The key text for the biblical understanding of marriage comes from the account of the creation of humanity in the first book of the Bible (Gn 2:24). This text is used by Jesus during a discussion about divorce (Mt 19:5; Mk 10:7-8) and then by the letter to the Ephesians when it speaks about the meaning of marriage (Eph 5:31). Coming from the origin, it reappears at critical moments in the reflection on marriage, a sign that it undoubtedly transmits something essential:

> For this reason a man will leave his father and mother and be united to his wife, and they will become one flesh.

---

[1] Although marriage as such is not specifically Christian, lifelong faithfulness in marriage is becoming harder and harder to achieve and justify outside of an explicit commitment linked to faith in Christ.

If we set this text alongside the words of Jesus on the family we examined earlier, an important parallel comes to light. Jesus says that whoever loves their father or mother more than him is not worthy of him (Mt 10:37); he says further that those who leave father and mother will receive infinitely more in the universal family of God (Mt 19:29). Now it is significant that the above text on marriage begins in exactly the same way. This should alert us to the fact that the turn of phrase has little or nothing to do with our parents as persons and the love we have for them. "Leaving one's father and mother" symbolizes rather the break with an old way of life which is necessary in order to begin a new existence. The person who marries thus repeats in a very concrete fashion the departure of Abraham which is the basis of the pilgrimage of faith (cf. Gn 12:1).

But just as for Abraham (Gn 12:2-3), as well as for Jesus on the way of the cross, this break with the old has meaning only as a road to a new life, a life of fullness. And, in the present case, this new life means joining another person to become one with him or her: "they will become one flesh." The word "flesh" here does not refer exclusively or primarily to sexuality; it stands for a total sharing of life, a belonging to the same family. The new life is, in a word, a life of communion. The newlyweds die to an "impersonal" existence as part of a collectivity, one for which they have not yet taken full responsibility, and they are then reborn as beings-in-relation. Marriage lived in its deepest dimension is thus a call to holiness. And like every relationship of holiness, this new life is fundamentally open. This openness is already prefigured on a biological level, since conjugal life normally leads to the birth of children and the formation of a new family.

Seen from this angle, marriage is shown to be a privileged way of being a person, of finding one's identity not in isolation but in a relationship of receiving and giving. That is why

Jesus replies to the Pharisees' question concerning divorce with this text from Genesis (Mt 19:1-9): if the marriage-commitment creates a new identity, gives a new name, it goes without saying that it is definitive. Here we are at the opposite extreme from any kind of legalistic outlook. It is essentially a question of taking into full account the requirements of personal life.

The biblical theology of marriage helps us to understand that it is not necessary to leave society and to live a life completely out of the ordinary in order to put into practice the radicalism of the Gospel. This radicalism can be expressed right at the heart of the world, by living *differently* the "normal" realities of human life. That is what Saint Paul is trying to explain in that controversial text which is the fifth chapter of the letter to the Ephesians. This passage offers a profound teaching about Christian marriage, one just as valuable today as it was then, but it takes as its starting-point marriage as it was practiced at the time, and for that reason those who come from another cultural context have a good amount of difficulty in understanding it. It would seem, for example, that the author counsels wives to "submit to their husbands" (Eph 5:22). Such a phrase is clearly calculated to cause any self-respecting contemporary woman to explode with indignation. Moreover, it feeds the myth, which unfortunately is considered "gospel truth" in some circles, of Paul the woman-hater, or even the hypocrite. After all, did he not write elsewhere that, in Christ, "there is no longer 'man and woman'" (Gal 3:28)?[2]

Let us begin by a preliminary clearing of the ground. To interpret a text correctly, we have to situate it in its original

---

[2] Regarding this verse, see the illuminating article of Anne-Marie Pelletier, "Il n'y a plus l'homme et la femme," *Communio* XVIII, 2 (March-April 1993), pp. 35-45.

context. Now if we place ourselves in the society of the time, the only one with which Paul was familiar, it quickly becomes evident that there is nothing polemical about the language he uses. Wives in those days were generally much younger than their husbands, had no education outside of the home, and essentially no role in public life. Inequality between men and women was a fact of life, and from the viewpoint of our world today this is a clear case of discrimination, of sexism, in short, something morally reprehensible. But a cultural phenomenon also needs to be taken into account: unlike modern societies which privilege "horizontal" relations of equality, the ancient world was much more at ease with "vertical" categories that organized life in different ranks. Its imagination was not democratic but hierarchical. In this context, a word like "submit" was not perceived as an act of violence. Saint Paul certainly had no intention of insulting or wounding the Christian wives to whom he was writing, nor to reject their just demands, and we have not a shred of evidence that they read him in this way.[3]

Inequality between the sexes, however, is not what the text is really talking about at all. We would make a grave error if we did not realize how deeply the letter to the Ephesians transforms this worldview from within. This transformation is expressed in two ways. Here is the context of the passage in question:

---

[3] In such a world, one's particular rights and responsibilities were a consequence of the place one occupied in the social hierarchy. And in that hierarchy one was inevitably situated between those "above" and those "below." Power flowed downward from the summit; one's own authority over others followed from one's submission to a higher authority. So what Paul's contemporaries would probably have heard in this injunction to "submit to your husbands" (even were this his main point, which we shall see it was not) was something like "take your rightful place in society." Cf. the Roman centurion's words in Luke 7:8: "I am a man placed under authority, with soldiers under me...." And cf. 1 Corinthians 11:10 where the married woman's head-covering is referred to as a "sign of authority."

> Do not get drunk on wine... but be filled with the Spirit
> ... submitting to one another out of respect (literally:
> fear) for Christ. Wives to their own husbands as to the
> Lord...   (Eph 5:18,21-22)

It should now be obvious that the alleged "submission" of wives is in fact a particular case of a general rule: *all* believers — women and men, the poor and the rich, the old and the young — are encouraged to submit to one another. This is underlined by the fact that, in the Greek original, the verb is not repeated, as the above translation makes clear. The question then arises: what does it mean here to "submit"? It is almost unthinkable that it refers to a perverse desire to let oneself be dominated or oppressed, to seek passivity by abdicating one's own will and blindly following a so-called authority-figure. A good methodology requires us to look for the meaning of the expression by comparing it to other similar exhortations in Saint Paul's letters:

> ...not [acting] with selfish ambition or conceit, but in
> humility each person considering the others superior
> to themselves, with each person not looking out for their
> own interests, but also for those of others.   (Ph 2:3-4;
>   cf. Rm 12:3,10; 1 Cor 9:19; 10:24,33; 1 P 5:5)[4]

Christian "submission" is nothing other than the basic principle that makes all community life of whatever sort possible — not looking out only or especially for oneself but realizing that we belong to one another and acting in consequence. And it goes without saying that this "submission" is nothing if it is not freely undertaken:

---

[4] Paul can refer in this regard to a teaching of Jesus himself which has left echoes in all four Gospels: Mt 20:25-28; Mk 10:42-45; Lk 22:24-27; Jn 13:13-15.

You have been called to freedom, my brothers and sisters, only don't let this freedom become a pretext for a self-centered existence (literally: for the flesh), but make yourselves slaves of one another out of love. (Gal 5:13)

The second way in which Paul modifies the mentality of his time is shown by the words he adds in Eph 5:22: "...as to the Lord." A wife's "submission" to her husband is thereby compared explicitly to a believer's "submission" to the crucified and risen Christ. This comparison makes even clearer that we are at the opposite extreme from any groveling or servile attitude. A baptized person "submits" to Christ by realizing that she has freely spoken a yes that from now on defines her new identity, a yes by which she has entered into a communion that gives meaning to her life and that renders futile any quest for a definitive meaning elsewhere. In analogous fashion (the parallel is evidently not perfect[5]), the author of Ephesians asks wives to realize that the meaning of their call to follow Christ cannot be separated from their relationship with their husbands. She is no longer on her own; she must take him into account in whatever she does.

And Christ, for his part, inserts the believer's "submission" into the greater and more inclusive "submission" that he himself has undertaken. A striking image of this is given in John's Gospel, by Jesus' act during the Last Supper. "The Teacher and Lord" gets up from the table and takes the role

---

[5] Among other things because, unlike Christ, husbands are not the "savior" of their wives (Eph 5:23). For a brilliant exegesis of this passage, which shows with all the necessary precision that here the term "submission" has no negative connotations but rather describes the active and free participation of the Christian wife in the new creation by analogy with the Church, the new Eve, see Stephen Francis Miletic, *"One Flesh": Eph 5.22-24, 5.31: Marriage and the New Creation*, Analecta Biblica 115 (Rome: Biblical Institute Press, 1988).

of a slave by washing his disciples' feet (Jn 13:1-17). In this way he expresses in symbolic fashion what he will do the following day when he gives his life for humankind in order to communicate the gift of holiness. Similarly, Saint Paul advises Christian husbands to undertake a similar "submission":

> Husbands, love your wives in the same way that Christ loved the Church: he gave himself up for her to make her holy.... (Eph 5:25-26)

Here we have left any socio-cultural conformity far behind. In the ancient world (but has anything changed in this regard?) it was far from being a normal practice to encourage men to give their lives for their wives. In short, the apostle's intention here is not to champion a dissymetrical relationship between husbands and wives, but to reflect upon diversity in the light of faith in Christ, in order to show how it can provide an opening for communion. In other words, Saint Paul starts from a sociological reality, marriage as it was concretely practiced in his day, and tries to demonstrate how it can be, for believers, a way of being persons in the image of Christ, beings who find their identity in a communion of life through the total gift of themselves made to another person.

It is in this context that we can grasp the authentic and deeply positive meaning of the biblical and Christian teaching concerning human sexuality. The contemporary world, founded to a great extent as it is upon a different vision of the human being, has trouble entering into an outlook so foreign to some of its most deeply held notions. And when the Church deals with this topic as if it were primarily a matter of laws and prohibitions, it only aggravates the misunderstanding and condemns itself to be viewed as a fossil, not to say an enemy of human self-fulfillment. To find a way out of this impasse, we must situate the topic in the global context of the biblical vision of the human being and of holiness. In other words, before we can talk about what we should *do*, we need to reach some understanding and consensus about who we *are* and what life is all about.

In all the civilizations of the ancient world, sexuality is closely attached to the realm of the sacred, of the holy. Wedded as it is to the enigma of the origins of life, it is not viewed as a reality that falls under the control of human beings but rather as a mystery beyond their ken. And in the mentality of traditional cultures, the mystery of life is one with the mystery of death. Modern biology, incidentally, confirms this intuition: on the threshold of life, a single-celled organism reproduces and dies by one and the same act.[6] But the modern world, with its utilitarian perspectives, has eliminated the category of the holy and favored fragmentation. Everything is now subject to manipulation by human beings. We have succeeded, if one can speak of success in this respect, in separating to an ever greater degree the conception and birth of a new human being from the sexual act, which as a result is determined largely by other criteria.

The ancient world, however, considered sexuality holy. A mysterious reality which comes from elsewhere, it both fascinated and frightened. We have already pointed out a tendency to hedge holy realities about with rules, both to protect them and to protect oneself from their disturbing power. And in this, the Hebrew Bible follows the pattern of most ancient civilizations: the sexual act, like all that pertains to birth and death, is circumscribed by a host of "laws of purity." These

---

[6] See also Jesus' reply to the Sadducees (Mt 22:30): where there is no longer death, there is no conjugal life either. See Cormier, *Généalogie de Personne*, pp. 82-83.

laws attempt to keep the mystery intact, so that people can benefit from its creative power while keeping its destructive potential under control.

We have also seen that not every society understands holiness — and therefore sexuality — in the same manner. It is sometimes seen as an impersonal energy, a blind force that human beings can channel and make use of by discovering and mastering the appropriate rites. These forces are sometimes symbolized by divine figures, fertility gods, although this changes the underlying dynamics very little. This was the case notably in the societies of Canaan in the midst of which the people of Israel lived. Agricultural civilizations with an extremely well developed cult of fertility, they placed even human sexuality, by means of ritual prostitution, at the service of the productivity of the soil, so essential for their survival.

From the very beginning, Israel opposed a clear refusal to every impersonal and magical way of viewing holiness. God alone is holy and cannot be manipulated. God is the source of all life and, as a result, a relationship with him is one of welcoming the divine blessings and responding with gratitude. This explains the horror with which God's people looked on the instrumentalization of sexuality in the cult of fertility. This antipathy was so strong that (sacred) prostitution quickly became in Israel the symbol *par excellence* of idolatry (cf. Ho 2:4,7; Jr 5:7-8; Is 1:21; Ezk 16; 23).

The evolution described in the Bible goes in the opposite direction from instrumentalization, toward an ever increasing *personalization* of sexuality. If the fire of holiness is to lead not to disintegration but rather to the full development of a person (cf. Ex 3:2), it must be part of a personal relationship. This means that sexuality finds its "natural" locus as part of a relationship based on a definitive commitment, where mutual receiving and giving can be lived out over time. A relationship, moreover, which is not turned inward in a kind of *égoïsme à deux* but which is open to welcome life, actualized on the physical level by the birth of children but naturally not limited to that. Only in this way does the language of the body not contradict what the being as a whole (the biblical "heart") intends to express; the instincts and the emotions are placed at the service of the person. Lived at the heart of a relationship where two beings commit themselves to becoming a single body by the total sharing of their lives, human sexuality does not become a force of dissolution but an incomparable energy of creation.[7]

This rapid survey will hopefully make at least one thing clear. Despite so many preconceived notions to the contrary, Saint Paul's teaching in the domain of conjugal life, and indeed the entire New Testament vision of sexuality, is not at all determined by a rejection of the physical side of life, as will sometimes later be the case due in part to the influence of Greek philosophy. The key is rather to be found in the notion of *consistency*. The important thing is to live a life that tends toward the greatest degree of coherence possible, toward the fullness of personal life. If Christians are persons who live "for the Lord," who are "one spirit with him," who "do not belong to themselves" but are "temples of the Holy Spirit" (1 Cor 6:13, 17,19), then what they express through their bodies should confirm this identity by being the transcription of a fully per-

---

[7] Pope John Paul II has reflected deeply on the personal roots of conjugal life seen in the light of the Bible. His personalistic outlook opens up surprising new perspectives for mainstream theology. See among other texts his Wednesday General Audiences from 1979 to 1981 in John Paul II, *The Theology of the Body: Human Love in the Divine Plan* (Boston: Pauline Books and Media, 1997), and the encyclical letter *Mulieris dignitatem* (15 August 1984). See also Mary G. Durkin, *Feast of Love: Pope John Paul II on Human Intimacy* (Chicago: Loyola University Press, 1983).

sonal commitment. Otherwise, as Saint Paul puts it in a particularly profound expression, they "sin against their own
bodies" (1 Cor 6:18), not according to some archaic notion
of ritual or physical defilement but because they are walking
along two roads at the same time; their life witnesses to a deep-
rooted split which militates against the unity of their being.

This being said, it must immediately be added that the
spirit of perfectionism has nothing in common with the Gospel. Personal unity is not forged in a day, or a year, but gradually, through successive approximations. In the delicate domain of the intimate life, perhaps more than elsewhere, there
is no room for rigidity and judgments without compassion,
especially when they are turned against oneself. The motive-
force of growth in personhood is not the inflexibility of the
human will but rather the inward presence of Holiness in
person, the Spirit of God, the Source of forgiveness, in other
words of a Love that always makes a new beginning possible.
With infinite patience, God makes use of whatever readiness
to change and grow he finds in us in order to lead us towards
inner unity. And so we can rely on the words of Saint John:
"If our hearts were to condemn us, ... God is greater than our
hearts and he knows everything" (1 Jn 3:20).

* * *

At the end of this long and somewhat digressive chapter, it may be useful to recover the thread of our reasoning.
Above all a personal reality, Christian holiness turns believers
into beings who find the meaning of their life in a communion. Through a relationship with Christ, they enter into the
same relationship which he has with the One he calls "Abba";
they become sons and daughters in the Son. And they trans-

late this new identity into a way of living with their fellow human beings, situating themselves within the universal family of God. The Church is nothing other than the expression of this family, called to be more and more inclusive until it identifies with the whole of humanity.

Equally far from being mere puppets or detached monads, baptized persons place their abilities and qualifications at the service of others. Knowing that everything they have has been bestowed on them, their deepest desire is to give in turn the gift they have received. By the different choices they make in the course of their lives, they try to live out the yes of their baptism by applying it to a specific situation. Among these different choices, two life-commitments occupy a special place: the commitments to marriage and to celibacy for Christ.

Today we are more aware than ever that marriage and consecrated celibacy are not the only possibilities of living out the Christian faith. There are as many ways of living "for God" and "for others" as there are persons. Starting from their own gifts and their own limits, everyone is called to allow their personal life to blossom, to discover their own freedom by accepting what God wishes for them in communion with their brothers and sisters, by giving themselves freely out of love. In our contemporary world, at the heart of rapidly evolving societies, it is to be expected that some people will not find exterior models that correspond exactly to what they are searching for, for example in living out a celibate lifestyle for the sake of Christ, or in discovering how to create a Christian home which is a "domestic church" at the heart of societies with quite different priorities. They need an abundance of imagination and courage to discover their own way, listening to the "whisper of silence" in their heart of hearts and seeking a confirmation of this in the community of believers. If the adventure of holiness is sometimes an arduous journey, it is nonetheless a source of inexpressible joy, the joy of setting out on the same road as Abraham and Moses, Mary and Peter, and a multitude of women and men down through the ages who entrusted their life to a Word that went before them, leading them onward like a pillar of fire.

Questions for Reflection

1. Read Matthew 6:24-34. What basic attitudes do we find in this text that follow from a life of communion with Christ? Does this text help us to understand the foundations and the meaning of Christian simplicity? How can we move towards greater simplicity of heart and of life, in our personal lives as well as in the life of our Christian communities?
2. The Christians of the first centuries sometimes called the family a "domestic church." What dimensions of the life of the Church can be lived out in miniature by a couple?
3. By what choices and lifestyle can someone who is not (or not yet) committed in marriage or by a vow of celibacy live out the yes of their baptism? How can this way of life be seen not as a time of waiting, still less as a last resort, but as a real and fully worthwhile way of living a holy life?

Conclusion

As we reach the end of our journey, let us dare to make a bold statement: God is much simpler than we are; in fact, God is simplicity itself. God is so simple that he has only one thought; God's sole desire is to create a communion of persons, in other words free beings whose life consists entirely in receiving and giving. The reason for this is just as simple: God *is* a communion of persons. We pray to a God who is Father, Son and Holy Spirit, thereby confessing our faith in the Trinity, but more often than not we do not understand the true import of this doctrine. God is not an isolated being. God is communion, being-in-relation. By becoming persons in communion, we are truly in the divine image.

If these are God's intentions, then how does he go about realizing them? First God creates a world, then he calls into existence beings capable of becoming persons in the divine image (cf. Gn 1:27). And in the world he has created, God places signs of his holiness, "burning bushes" that fascinate, that lure human beings away from the banality of everyday life and open before them new horizons, a space of freedom. It is true that this experience of holiness has a frightening side to it; it turns the world upside down, unsettling human beings who are always tempted to settle down comfortably amidst what they have acquired. But they have no need to be afraid: when they run the risk of approaching the fire of holiness, seekers will experience the happiness and the consolation of hearing a voice tell them, "Don't be afraid!" And they will discover a personal reality, a God who calls them by name and in so doing reveals to them what is most personal in themselves. Beyond all forms of conditioning and constraint, they will discover that they are free and are called in their turn to offer a response, to become responsible.

What we have just described does not happen in a single day, neither in the history of humanity nor in the life of each one of us. More often than not, without always realizing it, human beings look for excuses so as not to hear the call and have to respond. This obliges God, with tireless patience, to search constantly for new ways to touch the hearts of his creatures. And then one day, the response so long desired becomes a reality. The Bible reveals this encounter "in Spirit and truth" in the life of Mary, the mother of Jesus, and above all in Jesus himself — who is from all eternity the Son of God, the One whose entire existence is an attitude of welcome and response toward the Father's *eudokia*, the will of God's love.

Through the life of Jesus culminating in his death and resurrection, the possibility of being a person becomes fully accessible to us. We discover that God's call is at the same time a gift, the gift of God's Holiness in person, the Holy Spirit. For all who hold themselves open to this gift by a personal yes, recapitulated in the sacrament of baptism, the transfiguring fire is no longer something external. It sheds its warmth and light in the human heart, gradually consuming all forms of resistance to communion and making its bearer a being-in-relation who no longer belongs to himself. Baptized persons are henceforth fully at home only in the universal family of God, made concrete in a community with a universal outlook — the congregation of believers, the Church.

Need it be argued that such a vision of human beings as persons is far from being self-evident? Modern-day society offers us another image, diametrically opposed to this one. For the ruling belief-system, human beings are seen above all as individuals who create their own identity, beings who are their own source. On the road to self-realization, such beings will naturally feel the need of others. They will thus establish what it is customary to call "relationships" with their fellows. But this kind of gregariousness is of a different order than the personal relationships we have been talking about. Such "togetherness" lasts exactly as long as the individuals in question benefit from it, not one second longer. It does not change people in any real way, since their identity is not really implicated. It does not involve, in short, the dimension of *giving*, of *commitment*, whether in fact these words are spoken or not. And then, voices will of course arise to explain that this is the true meaning of the freedom desired by so many: an absence of ties, the highest degree of independence possible, the ability to do whatever I want whenever I please.

Since individuals as defined here can only count on themselves, the source of their security cannot be found in welcoming what comes from someone else. Rather than living in a reciprocal exchange with others, by receiving and giving, individuals inevitably attribute great importance to *possessing;* they can only be really sure about what they own. You are what you have, and so it is essential to accumulate all kinds of visible and invisible possessions to defend oneself against the chilling fate of losing one's identity, and even one's life.

For centuries in the West, such a vision of the human being had an overwhelmingly positive connotation. The "self-made man" was even seen as the summit of human evolution. Particularly predominant first in the Anglo-Saxon and Protestant world, especially as a result of the two periods of cultural upheaval known as the Renaissance/Reformation and the Enlightenment, this tendency exercises its fascination wherever people begin to free themselves from traditional fetters. One could say that it has become practically synonymous with what is called modernity. In one sense, the individual is a product of modernity. A caricature of the person, it presupposes an awakening of the free and responsible subject as a result of a personal encounter. Except for a handful of exceptions, a traditional society is peopled neither by individuals nor by persons as we have described them here, but by beings who for the most part are still embedded in a collectivity with its customs and pre-established roles.

The modern world, however, exalts the individual, a bit like an adolescent exhilarated by his first sallies into the world of adults, whose newfound capacities convince him that he has already attained maturity, that happiness and fulfillment are there for the taking. For some time now, however, our contemporaries have become more and more aware of the other side of the coin. The individual self is unable to keep its promises, to fulfill its tasks; its flaws more and more meet the eye. The transition to a post-modern society can be defined as simultaneous with the breakup of the modern self. For the moment, unfortunately, no true alternative has imposed itself. Attempts to celebrate a post-modern lifestyle, the flexible and enterprising "protean self,"[1] seem to be premature; most of our

---

[1] See Introduction, note 3.

contemporaries are still painfully making their way amidst the debris of individualism.

This extremely modern picture is in reality quite old, because in the final analysis it is rooted in the human heart. In the well-known parable of the prodigal son, Jesus draws a perfect portrait of an individual as we have described him. It is not surprising that the being in question is an adolescent:

> A man had two sons. The younger said to his father, "Father, give me my portion of the inheritance." So he split up his property between them. A few days later, the younger son took all his fortune and set out for a far-away land.... (Lk 15:11-13)

"Give me what belongs to me." Not satisfied with living in the father's house, the younger son wants to take exclusive possession of what is his. Proud of his autonomy, he takes his property and goes off alone. Do we not have here in a nutshell a poignant image of the human race in its relations with God? If Jesus tells this story, it is because he knows that in each of us there is an individual, and he wants us to realize that this is not the way to true happiness. We are not meant to blame the prodigal son, but rather to examine his behavior and learn the lesson for our individual and collective lives.

And then, at the end of the parable, Jesus gives us a marvelous description of a person. It is found in the words which the father speaks to his other son. Although the elder brother remained physically present in his father's house, he did not understand any better the meaning of the relationship. So much for the notion that it is by mere outward conformity that we will somehow earn divine favor. In any event, to be a person in the image of Christ means hearing God say these words to us:

"My child, you are always with me, and all that is mine
is yours."   (Lk 15:31)

These words take up Christ's own experience at his baptism, which becomes ours when we set out in his footsteps:
"You are my beloved Son; on you my favor rests" (Mk 1:11).
We realize then that there is nothing to be afraid of, we have
been created for communion.

The distinction between an individual and a person can
also be understood by reflecting on the difference between a
mask and an *icon*. When we feel alone and vulnerable, we tend
instinctively to hide behind a mask, to play a preset role. In a
traditional society, everything is a mask, a social role, but this
is not perceived as a constraint. Individuals, however, while
feeling that the roles they play are artificial because they do
not correspond to their inner self, use them to fence off a
private space where they can be free, like a mask which acts
as a barrier to protect them from the eyes of others who are
viewed as hostile.

But the price paid for this stratagem is high. A mask keeps
us from entering into authentic relations with our fellows. In
addition, it remains immobile and finally becomes a prison
which stifles all growth and change. When a mask becomes
unbearable, the usual solution is to take it off and exchange
it for another one. But if one day the fatal question arises,
"Who am I?", then the only answer one will be able to give is,
"I am a collection of masks."

We are not far here from what the Bible calls an idol:

When the people saw that Moses was so long in coming
down from the mountain, they gathered round Aaron
and said, "Come, make us gods who will go before us.
As for this fellow Moses who brought us up out of Egypt,
we don't know what has happened to him."   (Ex 32:1)

Because they are afraid, the people want to replace their trust in an invisible God with a reality accessible to the eyes and the hand. Aaron makes a golden statue in the form of a calf. But this kind of "god" doesn't work at all. It cannot go before the people and lead them anywhere, certainly not towards the fullness of life, because in the final analysis it is nothing but a projection of their own insecurity. And do we not all have our "golden calves," which can take a host of different names depending on the occasion?

An icon is something of a completely different order. If, in looking at an icon, we focus above all on the painter's skill, the delicacy of his line, his choice of colors, not only have we not understood the essential, but we are in the process of getting off the track. As opposed to an art object destined for aesthetic contemplation, an icon has been defined as "a window open on infinity." By means of a visible reality, it wants to permit us to enter into a relationship with the invisible Mystery. In this respect, it occupies a place analogous to the humanity of Christ. The first icon, in fact, is the face of Christ, "image (in Greek: *eikōn*) of the invisible God" (Col 1:15). The primordial quality of an icon is its *transparency:* rather than capturing the eyes and riveting them on itself, it attempts to attract our glance and immediately lead it on further, toward the unimaginable Source.

Christ's call and the gift of the Holy Spirit invite us to bring to fulfillment the promise contained in our creation, that of being a person in the image of God. In these pages, I have tried to show that a relationship with God causes us to die to an individual, isolated existence in order to be reborn as persons in communion. Thus all together, as the Church, we become an icon of the God who is Trinity. Beyond our words and perhaps without our even realizing it, it is this icon which will speak to humankind and give it a glimpse of the breathtaking beauty of a communion in God.

Such an undertaking is not the fruit of our own efforts but rather a consequence of God's holiness in us. The Holy Spirit guides us along the way which was Christ's. Better still, he guides us on the way which *is* Christ (Jn 14:6). In the final analysis, holiness in a human life consists in this: letting the fire of the Spirit transfigure our lives in order to make us more and more transparent to its light and its heat. In this way our life together will become a burning bush able to fascinate a world thirsting for truth and love. It will radiate an energy of compassion that attracts without compelling, that unifies without excluding, that opens at the heart of a world in the process of passing away a permanent space of freedom, that of a communion of persons.

Questions for Reflection

1. Read Luke 19:1-10. How do I respond to God's call by taking on responsibilities for others? Who am I responsible for? How do I express this responsibility? Where do I find the strength to do so?
2. What are some of our individual and collective "golden calves" (Ex 32:1ff.)? What gives us the courage to abandon them, to take off our masks?
3. What aspects of the life of the Church make it an icon of the Trinity? What veils its true face? How can we restore this face?